PRAISE FOR
The Measure of a Woman

The Measure of a Woman is a basic beauty essential for every woman. Through this book, the Word of God and biblical examples, we see the standard for the perspective, image, communication and relationships of a godly woman.

AMIE DOCKERY
Author, *On Daddy's Shoulders* and *Designing Your Dream Husband*

Gene and Elaine Getz's book *The Measure of a Woman* is a wonderful resource for Christian women in every phase of life. This biblically based book is instructive and presents questions with each chapter that will challenge you to consider your responses to life's situations and encourage you to set goals for spiritual growth. Thank you, Gene and Elaine. Your work is appreciated!

ANNA HAYFORD

Gene and Elaine have done it again! *The Measure of a Woman* is pertinent, powerful and practical. The biblical principles shared in this book offer every woman—no matter what stage of life—encouragement, wisdom and tools to grow in grace as a woman of God. From Bible passages to life experiences, and from Greek word studies to personal heart-to-heart letters written by incredible women, each after God's own heart, *The Measure of a Woman* is a must-read for every woman who desires to break free from the bondage of the world's standards and realize God's true measure of a woman.

DEBBIE HEYDRICK
Author, *I'll Hold You in Heaven Remembrance Book*
Founder, Angels in Heaven Ministries

The Measure of a Woman confronts the questions that women are asking and provides straightforward, meaningful answers from God's Word.

CAROLE LEWIS
Author, *The Mother-Daughter Legacy*
National Director, First Place

The Measure of a Woman

Gene A. Getz and Elaine A. Getz

Regal

From Gospel Light
Ventura, California, U.S.A.

Regal

PUBLISHED BY REGAL BOOKS
FROM GOSPEL LIGHT
VENTURA, CALIFORNIA, U.S.A.
PRINTED IN THE U.S.A.

Regal Books is a ministry of Gospel Light, a Christian publisher dedicated to serving the local church. We believe God's vision for Gospel Light is to provide church leaders with biblical, user-friendly materials that will help them evangelize, disciple and minister to children, youth and families.

It is our prayer that this Regal book will help you discover biblical truth for your own life and help you meet the needs of others. May God richly bless you.

For a free catalog of resources from Regal Books/Gospel Light, please call your Christian supplier or contact us at 1-800-4-GOSPEL *or* www.regalbooks.com.

Library of Congress Cataloging-in-Publication Data
Getz, Gene A.
 The measure of a woman / Gene A. Getz and Elaine A. Getz.
  p. cm.
 Includes bibliographical references.
 ISBN 0-8307-3286-1
 1. Christian women—Religious life. 2. Wives—Religious life. I. Getz, Elaine A. II. Title.
 BV4527.G467 2004
 248.8'43—dc22   2004010056

1   2   3   4   5   6   7   8   9   10   /   10   09   08   07   06   05   04

Rights for publishing this book in other languages are contracted by Gospel Light Worldwide, the international nonprofit ministry of Gospel Light. Gospel Light Worldwide also provides publishing and technical assistance to international publishers dedicated to producing Sunday School and Vacation Bible School curricula and books in the languages of the world. For additional information, visit www.gospellightworldwide.org; write to Gospel Light Worldwide, P.O. Box 3875, Ventura, CA 93006; or send an e-mail to info@gospellightworldwide.org.

Contents

Acknowledgments

We would like to thank in a very special way 11 wonderful women we've served with at Fellowship Bible Church North in Plano, Texas. All of them have functioned faithfully as elders' wives, beautifully demonstrating the qualities outlined by Paul in his letter to Titus. They have also contributed to this new edition by reflecting in letter form their thoughts about the characteristics of maturity described here. Their names are as follows:

Maureen Burford

Linda Cole

Sharon Cornwall

Joan Craig

Barbara Debenport

Ellen Ellwood

Shannon Hansen

Clarice Harris

Charlotte Lindgren

Mary Logue

Joyce Saffel

We're also deeply indebted to Iva Morelli and Sue Mitchell for their invaluable assistance in preparing this book for publication. They too are women of character. They both serve faithfully in the Center for Church Renewal and the ministry of Renewal Radio.

A Mentoring Model

Today, we hear a lot about mentoring—which, of course, implies having a mentor. Have you ever been asked the question, Would you be my mentor? Or perhaps you're the one who has asked this question.

This concept evolved from Greek mythology and originally referred to Mentor, Odysseus's trusted counselor. Eventually the term was used to refer to any wise and trusted counselor or teacher.

Clearly, the terms "mentor" and "mentoring" have roots that go back thousands of years. But of greater importance is the fact that mentoring is a biblical concept that is beautifully outlined in Paul's letter to Titus when Titus, then a young man, was stationed on the island of Crete to help establish new churches. In one succinct but power-packed paragraph, Paul outlined both the mentoring process and the goals for this process, particularly as mentoring relates to women:

> Likewise, *teach the older women* to be reverent in the way they live, not to be slanderers or addicted to much wine, but to teach what is good. *Then they can train the younger women* to love their husbands and children, to be self-controlled and pure, to be busy at home, to be kind, and

to be subject to their husbands, so that no one will malign the word of God (Titus 2:3-5).

As we'll see in this study, some of the older women Paul referred to may have been God-fearing Jews or converts to Judaism before they became Christians. In fact, some may have actually put their faith in Jesus Christ as their Messiah on the Day of Pentecost, a little over 30 years before Paul and Titus brought the gospel message to Crete (see Acts 2:1,5,11).

However, many of the young women living on this island had converted to Jesus Christ only a short time earlier from a purely pagan lifestyle, the values of which reflected the decadence of the deteriorating Roman Empire rather than the laws of God that were delivered at Mount Sinai.

In order to help these younger women become more mature believers, Paul instructed Titus to focus first on older women, teaching them how to demonstrate the fruit of the Holy Spirit. These women, in turn, were to train (mentor) the younger women to also "live a life worthy of the calling [they had] received" (Eph. 4:1).

We first prepared this material for publication when we began our church-planting efforts by starting the first Fellowship Bible Church in Dallas, Texas, in the early 1970s. And though in this completely new edition the outline remains the same as it appeared in Paul's God-inspired letter to Titus, we've completely rewritten and updated each chapter for the twenty-first century. Our prayer now is that this new edition will continue what Paul and Titus began in their church-planting ministry nearly 2,000 years ago—equipping women to be all God intended them to be! May this book assist you in reproducing, in many respects, Paul's mentoring model for years to come.

CHAPTER I

Gaining God's Perspective on Beauty

A Cultural Portrait of Sensuality Gone Wild

We live in a culture that is obsessed with the external. The next time you approach the checkout counter at any major food mart, note the titles of women's magazines. Go a step further and scan the titles of articles in these various publications. For example, here are a few that you may find: "Get an Amazing Body," "Flirty Skirts, Slinky Tops," "Better Skin, Hair, Sex," "Sexy Cuts and Styles." Even teen magazines for young girls focus on physical appearance. Here are titles from three different publications: "795 Ways to Look Amazing," "419 Ways to Look Pretty," "476 Ways to Look Sexy."

There's no question that we're living in a culture obsessed with *how* a woman looks. The word "sexy" has almost become a synonym for "beautiful" and "attractive"—particularly in describing a woman's appearance. In television commercials, whether a company is selling shampoo or automobiles, sex sells, and the focus is often a sensuous woman.

No organized group has capitalized on this obsession more than the music industry. Though men have joined the parade of exhibitionists in live concerts and on music videos, young women are still the major sex objects. Unfortunately, their female fans attempt to imitate what they see on TV, in the movies and in live concerts.

Tragic Consequences

This obsession with external beauty among young women has for some become a psychological and physical tragedy. Never before in our society have we seen more cases of anorexia and bulimia. Young women have become obsessed with *how they look* rather than *who they are.*

This tragedy involves even broader distortions. Many women actually believe that how they look to men is the key to their own happiness. Unfortunately, many men are also self-deceived, believing that a woman's external beauty is the key to their own personal fulfillment in life. Sadly, Hugh Hefner and his ilk are perpetuating this myth—in themselves and in the women who have also bought into this destructive lie.

Beautiful Eve—Astonished Adam

On the other hand, we mustn't use this obsession with physical attractiveness to negate both the reality and the importance of external beauty. After all, when God created Eve and presented her to Adam, what Adam *saw* was perfection—which certainly included Eve's physical features. Loosely translated, Adam's reaction when he saw this exquisite gift from God was "Wow!" C. F. Keil and F. Delitzsch point out that the Hebrew language captures his "joyous astonishment."[1] Though he exclaimed, "This is now bone of my bones and flesh of my flesh" (Gen. 2:23), Eve was also uniquely different and beautiful. She was a woman—God's special gift to Adam.

Obviously, Adam was attracted to Eve's external beauty. After all, they "were both naked, and they felt no shame" (Gen. 2:25). They were guilt free. But what Adam experienced that day was more than physical attraction and what Eve portrayed was far more than sexy. Her beauty included her psychological and spiritual nature. She along with Adam was made in the image of God. And since God is Spirit and void of physical features, she reflected who God is.

She was a living soul manifesting an inner loveliness that came from God's invisible qualities—and when Adam exclaimed his approval, he saw more than outward characteristics as we so often describe them today. They were soul mates in the truest sense of the word.

A Paradise Lost

Sadly, this God-created perfection was terribly marred and distorted when Eve was overcome with temptation and ate the forbidden fruit. When Adam followed suit, they suddenly saw each other in a different light. In fact, they both "realized they were naked; so they sewed fig leaves together and made coverings for themselves" (Gen. 3:7).

Guilt and Shame

However, what they then experienced was more than feelings of modesty. Guilt and shame entered the human race. Their relationship with God was affected. The intimate fellowship they had enjoyed with their creator turned into a desire to hide from God—not just physically, but spiritually. Sin had taken its toll, impacting their relationship not only with God but also with one another. The Bible explains and history demonstrates that what happened that day in the Garden of Eden has negatively impacted male and female relationships even to this day. God spoke directly to Eve, but the words He spoke addressed how sin would impact both men and women:

> To the woman he said, "I will greatly increase your pains in childbearing; with pain you will give birth to children. Your desire will be for your husband, and he will rule over you" (Gen. 3:16).

Conflict and Tension

Hebrew scholar Ron Allen, in his excellent book entitled *The Majesty of Man*, captured the real meaning of God's statements:

> God then spoke to the woman as a consequence of her rebellion against the beneficent rule of Yahweh, the following new realities that shall mark her life: I will bring something new into the wonder of the bringing of children into the world. I will greatly magnify your pain in giving birth. When you give birth to your children it will be in physical pain. I will also allow pain to come into your marriage relationship with your husband. You will tend to desire to usurp the role I have given to him as the compassionate leader in your home, rejecting his role and belittling his manhood. And the man on his part will

tend to relate to you in loveless tyranny, dominating and stifling your integrity as an equal partner to himself.[2]

God, of course, did not suddenly remove Eve's physical beauty or Adam's manly features after they sinned. But at that moment, they both experienced the curse of death—both physically and spiritually. The aging process would eventually lead to the grave. "For dust you are [God said] and to dust you will return" (Gen. 3:19).

Beauty—Blessing or Curse?

Regarding a woman's continual physical beauty, this God-created gift was destined to become both a blessing and a curse. On the one hand, it would become a wonderful asset—at least temporarily—enabling most women to feel good about themselves and to be admired by Adam's kind. On the other hand, a woman's physical beauty would often make her no more than a sex object in the eyes of many men.

Sarai's Beauty Beheld

Consider the biblical story. It was Sarai's beauty—even at age 75—that got both her and Abram into serious trouble with the king of Egypt. In fact, the biblical record is very specific: "When Abram came to Egypt, the Egyptians saw that she was a very beautiful woman. And when Pharaoh's officials saw her, they praised her to Pharaoh, and she was taken into his palace" (Gen. 12:14-15).

Abram had anticipated this reaction. As they were about to cross the border into Egypt, he turned to Sarai—paying her a great tribute! "I know what a *beautiful woman* you are. When the Egyptians see you, they will say, 'This is his wife.' Then they will kill me but will let you live. Say you are my sister, so that I will be treated well for your sake and my life will be spared because of you" (Gen. 12:11-13). Eventually God bailed both Abram and Sarai out of this mess, but the point is this: Sin did not suddenly destroy Sarai's physical beauty—but she *did* become a sex object in the eyes of a group of pagan men.

Bathsheba's Beauty Bath

This distortion was not limited to unbelievers in the biblical story. Let's not forget David, a man after God's own heart! One evening, obviously restless and unable to sleep because his soldiers had gone off to war, he got out of bed and paced back and forth on his palace roof. And what should grab his attention but a "very beautiful" woman bathing (2 Sam. 11:2). Even though Bathsheba was married to one of David's most trusted soldiers, he sent for her, committed adultery and fathered an illegitimate child.

Again the point is clear! Sin did not suddenly mar Bathsheba's physical features or David's capacity to respond to her sensual beauty—but in a moment of temptation and lust, this very attractive woman became a sex object. Both David and Bathsheba were impacted by the sin of Adam and Eve.

Tamar's Beauty Disguised

David paid a great price for his sin. No doubt one of the most tragic results involved his son Amnon, who raped Tamar, one of David's own daughters. The biblical record describes this young woman as "the *beautiful sister* of Absalom" (2 Sam. 13:1). Amnon was so enamored by Tamar's physical attributes that he tricked her and disgraced her. And at this point, we see another result of sin: Amnon's lust turned to hate! (see 2 Sam. 13:15).

The Impact of Sin

There is no question that sin impacted Adam and Eve at two levels: their relationship with God and with one another. Furthermore, it impacted a woman's role in a very specific way. Her beauty would be one of her greatest assets but also one of her greatest liabilities. In fact, not only would she become a sex object because of the way sin impacted men, but she also would soon discover that she could use her sensual charms to manipulate and control the opposite sex both to achieve her own selfish goals and to express her anger and frustration. Ask a prostitute how she feels about men, and if she's honest, she'll more than likely tell you that she resents them—often because as a young girl she was sexually abused by a father, an uncle or another male in the close family or neighborhood circle.

A Journey into Lesbianism

Anne Paulk was a typical little girl. However, when she was about four years old, a teenaged boy in her neighborhood abused her sexually. Warned by this predator never to tell her parents or anyone what happened, Anne reaped a lot of self-inflicted pain because of her silence. For one thing, she became a tomboy because she didn't feel protected as a girl. This unfortunate sexual experience kept her from embracing femininity, leaving her weak and vulnerable to homosexual experiences.

Eventually, Anne became a Christian and left this lifestyle. Today she is happily married with children of her own. But her story illustrates the results of sin, particularly at the hands of a young man who acted out his sinful impulses and desperately wounded a little girl who has suffered the consequences even to this day.[3]

Heterosexual Vulnerability

Think for a moment how many young women today fall prey to the human predicament that began so many centuries ago in the Garden of Eden. Many in our own culture willingly succumb to a young man's aggressive passions, thinking that if they give in to a sexual experience, they'll be loved and accepted.

Unfortunately, some young women actually believe they'll continue to be attractive to those who seduce them—which, of course, is another result of sin. Rationalization began in the Garden and continues to this day! Sadly, the ready availability of abortion has only complicated the result of sin, leading to guilt, anger and other emotional and psychological complications.

The true measure of a woman involves beauty that is far more than skin deep.

What Is True Beauty?

We must realize and understand that the true measure of a woman involves beauty that is far more than skin deep. It involves that unique quality that characterized Eve before sin entered the world—the image of God. The apostle Peter referred to this attribute as an "unfading beauty" (1 Pet. 3:4). It certainly does not exclude physical beauty, but the implication is clear: When physical beauty fades, there is a beauty that will last! More specifically, Peter described this beauty as "a gentle and quiet spirit" (v. 4), which represents one very important manifestation of the image of God.

Peter described this beauty as coming from the "inner self" (v. 4) and warned against the superficiality of external beauty— "outward adornment, such as braided hair and the wearing of gold jewelry and fine clothes" (v. 3). But don't misunderstand his meaning! Because of this statement in Scripture, there are some Christians who believe and teach that any form of outward adornment is inappropriate. To conclude that Peter was teaching that it's wrong for a woman to enhance her natural beauty is to miss the whole point. God's gift of external beauty *is* important to a man, and it's not wrong to use it as a means of pleasing the one you truly love and are committed to in marriage.

Read the Song of Songs. Consider also God's instructions in Proverbs:

> May your fountain be blessed, and may you rejoice in the *wife of your youth.* A loving doe, a graceful deer—may her breasts satisfy you always, may you ever be captivated by her love (Prov. 5:18-19).

Though this scriptural passage graphically describes a woman's physical beauty and its importance in a marriage relationship, Peter emphasized that a wife's physical attractiveness alone will never endure as a means of pleasing her husband. In fact, without inner beauty, external beauty can quickly become superficial. It's a woman's inner attractiveness that endures and wins respect over the years. It's also this inner grace that makes external qualities even more attractive. And when physical beauty fades because of the aging process, it's a woman's internal qualities that will stand the test of time.

A Beautiful Woman—God's Perspective

When Paul wrote his letter to Titus, he recorded the most comprehensive list of qualities for measuring a woman's character and true beauty that we can find any place in the New Testament. The apostle had left this young missionary pastor on the island of Crete to establish the churches that they had just planted. First, Paul outlined the qualifications for elders and overseers, those who would manage and shepherd local groups of believers (Titus 1:5-9). Second, he described a profile for recognizing maturity in older men generally (2:1-2). Third—and the focus of our study—Paul exhorted Titus to teach the *older women* how to live so that they in turn could train the *younger women* to live out qualities of life that reflected inner beauty and that had the potential to be unfading as these women grew older (2:3-5).

Paul's character profile for women found in this short yet powerful epistle forms the outline for chapters 2 through 12 in *The Measure of a Woman.*

	Likewise, teach the older women
Chapter 2	*to be reverent in the way they live,*
Chapter 3	*not to be slanderers or*
Chapter 4	*[not to be] addicted to much wine, but*
Chapter 5	*to teach what is good.*
	Then they can train the younger women
Chapter 6	*to love their husbands and*
Chapter 7	*[to love their] children,*
Chapter 8	*to be self-controlled and*
Chapter 9	*[to be] pure,*
Chapter 10	*to be busy at home,*
Chapter 11	*to be kind, and*
Chapter 12	*to be subject to their husbands, so that no one will malign the word of God.*

God's Provision

Before we take a closer look at this inner beauty, it's important to consider God's provision for developing these internal qualities. I'm speaking of the Lord Jesus Christ. He came into this world to redeem us and to set us free from sin's curse. Though the most important aspect of this freedom involves eternal life, when we put our faith in Jesus Christ for salvation, He also sets us free to become more and more like God Himself. In a unique way, our creator's image that was marred when Adam and Eve sinned can be greatly restored. Our minds and hearts can be renewed. We can begin the process of spiritual and psychological restoration, which is absolutely essential for possessing inner beauty.

Thinking and Growing Together

The following questions are designed for group discussion after reading and studying the content of this chapter:

- How does our culture's obsession with a woman's external beauty affect women?
- How does this obsession negatively affect male-female relationships?
- Why do so many women buy into this lie?
- How can a woman focus on internal beauty without neglecting her outward appearance?
- If you feel comfortable, share how this emphasis on external beauty has affected you personally.

Set a Goal

Write out one goal you'd like to achieve as a result of this discussion.

CHAPTER 2

Reflecting God's Character

To be reverent in the way they live

TITUS 2:3

A Biblical Portrait of Phoebe's Exemplary Lifestyle

Though Paul's reference to this woman is very brief, it's amazing what we can learn about the way she lived her life as a Christian. Here are Paul's words:

> I commend to you our sister Phoebe, a servant of the church in Cenchrea. I ask you to receive her in the Lord in a way worthy of the saints and to give her any help she may need from you, for she has been a great help to many people, including me (Rom. 16:1-2).

A Typical Gentile City

Note that Paul identified Phoebe's hometown as Cenchrea, which is located just seven miles from Corinth. Like Corinth, Cenchrea was a Roman city permeated with pagan practices. Describing Gentile behavior in his letter to the Ephesians, Paul pulled no punches:

> They are darkened in their understanding and separated from the life of God because of the ignorance that is in them due to the hardening of their hearts. Having lost all sensitivity, they have given themselves over to sensuality so as to indulge in every kind of impurity, with a continual lust for more (Eph. 4:18-19).

Pagan Roots

Phoebe probably became a Christian during Paul's extended ministry in Corinth (see Acts 18:1-18). Interestingly, her name is the feminine form of "Phoibos," a name given to the god Apollo.[1] In other words, Phoebe had been converted from a pagan lifestyle, although like many Gentiles, she may have initially become God-fearing because of her association with God-fearing Jews.

A Trip to Rome

At some point in time, Phoebe traveled to Rome and when Paul wrote his letter to the Christians living in this imperial city and extended a series of greetings, Phoebe was literally at the top of the list (see Rom. 16:1). In fact, some believe that Phoebe actually carried Paul's letter to the Roman Christians, demonstrating how much Paul trusted this godly woman. This indeed would have been an awesome responsibility.

Think about it. How would you feel if you had been asked by the apostle Paul to deliver one of his personal letters that was inspired by the Holy Spirit? As you boarded a ship in Corinth and set sail for Rome, you would have kept this sacred scroll in your possession at all times. And as you disembarked near Rome, perhaps at Puteoli, and traveled by foot via the Appian Way (as Paul did later, see Acts 28:11-16), you would have felt an even greater burden to complete this sacred trust.

A Transformed Life

Paul wanted everyone in Rome to know that Phoebe had helped him personally. How, we're not told, but we can assume she came alongside him in a very special way when he ministered in Corinth—perhaps offering her home in Cenchrea as a place to stay or as a place where the believers in that city could worship.

Without question, Phoebe was reverent in the way she lived. Whatever her lifestyle as a pagan, as a Christian she no longer lived "as the Gentiles do, in the futility of their thinking" (Eph. 4:17). She had "put on the new self, created to be like God in true righteousness and holiness" (Eph. 4:24).

A Faithful Servant

Phoebe definitely developed a good reputation in the Christian community. Not only did she help Paul but she helped many others as well. In fact, some believe this godly woman had an official position in the church in Cenchrea, serving as a deacon. In Romans 16:1, Paul used the Greek word *diakonos* to describe Phoebe's ministry. This word, translated "servant" in the *New International Version* of the Bible, is also used to describe what *all* believers are to be and do. But in this passage Paul seemed to use the term in a more specific way: to describe her deacon role.

Paul went on to describe Phoebe as being *"worthy* of the saints" (v. 2), which means that she had earned the right to be highly respected and consequently to be cared for financially. In fact, she may have been a widow who met all of the qualifications also outlined by Paul in his first letter to Timothy (see 1 Tim. 5:9-10). If so, we can understand more fully why Paul recommended that the church in Rome should without hesitation "give her any help she may need" (Rom. 16:2).

Though Phoebe's role as Paul's assistant was very unique in this first-century setting, her character was not to be unique among women who professed to follow Jesus Christ. She beautifully exemplifies the quality Paul listed first in his letter to Titus: She was reverent in the way she lived.

A Woman's Reflections

Over the years, we've had the wonderful opportunity of ministering together with the wives of elders at Fellowship Bible Church North in Plano, Texas. We've asked each of these women to write a letter to you, the reader, reflecting on the qualities of maturity outlined by Paul in his letter to Titus.

In this chapter, it's a privilege to introduce you to Sharon Cornwall, who is serving our church along with her husband, Mike.

Dear Reader,

The portrait on Phoebe's life reminds me of a woman I'll call Sue. She and her husband were in our small group at church. To get to know one another, my husband and I encouraged everyone to relate his or her life story.

As Sue began to share, tears streamed down her face. "You

might not like me after I share my life," she said, straining to get the words out.

Sue had come out of a hard drug culture, and immorality was part of her lifestyle. We could feel her pain as she shared the results of bad choices. But we now saw God's amazing grace reflected in Sue's life! We told her so. We reassured her that she was cleansed and that Jesus was shining through! Her life was now being lived in devotion to God and in service to others. She, as Phoebe, proved herself reverent by her inner life, which was manifested outwardly.

As you conclude this chapter, ask yourself what God is seeking to do in your own life. Do you recognize the changes He has already made in your life? On the other hand, are there areas that need a "housecleaning" by the Holy Spirit? Ask God to reveal these to you, to give you a tender heart and then to empower you! He will! Your reverent life, lived for God and for others, will be both amazing and rewarding!

Lovingly yours,
Sharon Cornwall

The Way We Live

The Greek word Paul used, which is translated as "reverent," comes from *hieros,* meaning holy. In fact, this is the term Paul used to describe the Word of God when he wrote his final letter to Timothy. He reminded his "son in the faith" (1 Tim. 1:2) that he had become a Christian because his mother Eunice had laid the groundwork by teaching him "the *holy* [hieros] Scriptures" from the time he was a young child (2 Tim. 3:15).

You Are a Letter from Christ

Someone once said that our lives may be the only Bible some people will ever read. Paul underscored the importance of this idea when he wrote to the Corinthians:

> You yourselves are our letter, written on our hearts, known and read by everybody. You show that you are a letter from Christ, the result of our ministry, written not with ink but with the Spirit of the living God, not on tablets of stone but on tablets of human hearts (2 Cor. 3:2-3).

This is a very important truth. We cannot expect others to hear what we say unless they first see it demonstrated in our own lives. As a young man himself, Titus could not expect other younger men to respond to his teaching unless they saw it exemplified in his own life. That is why Paul wrote, "In everything set them an *example* by doing what is good" (Titus 2:7). In the same way, older women could not expect younger women to hear what they taught verbally unless they themselves were consistently reverent in the way they lived. In essence, they were to reflect the life of Jesus Christ.

Two-Dimensional Communication

Modeling is a foundational concept in New Testament communication. In actuality, Paul exemplified a twofold teaching approach in his own life-on-life ministry—modeling Christlikeness while verbally instructing believers. When he wrote to the Thessalonians, he reminded them of the way he, Silas and Timothy had utilized these two dimensions in their communication.

> **Their model:** "You are witnesses, and so is God, of how *holy, righteous* and *blameless* we were among you who believed" (1 Thess. 2:10).

Their teaching ministry: "For you know that we dealt with each of you as a father deals with his own children, *encouraging, comforting* and *urging* you to live lives worthy of God, who calls you into his kingdom and glory" (1 Thess. 2:11-12).

When Paul encouraged Timothy to communicate the Word of God faithfully to the Ephesians, he emphasized the same twofold approach:

His model: "Don't let anyone look down on you because you are young, but set an *example* for the believers in speech, in life, in love, in faith and in purity" (1 Tim. 4:12).

His teaching ministry: "Until I come, devote yourself to the public *reading* of Scripture, to *preaching* and to *teaching*" (1 Tim. 4:13; see also Titus 2:7-8).

Process Versus Perfection

When Paul wrote to Titus and instructed him to teach the older women to be reverent in the way they lived, this modeling was to embody all of the qualities Paul outlined for both older and younger women (see Titus 2:3-5). On the one hand, he was certainly not describing and demanding perfection. However, he was teaching the importance of consistency and a level of maturity that will win the respect of those we are attempting to lead. This is also why Paul emphasized that elders who are to shepherd the church are to "be above reproach" (1 Tim. 3:2) and "blameless" (Titus 1:6). In essence, they too were to be reverent in the way they lived so as to both model and teach Christlike character to others.

Don't let this standard intimidate or discourage you. Developing this kind of reputation in the Christian community takes time. Imagine how long it took Phoebe to grow in her relationship with Christ. It certainly didn't happen overnight. Remember that Paul ministered in Corinth for more than a year, and when he wrote his first letter to these believers, he accused most of them of still being "infants in Christ" (1 Cor. 3:1). They were "still worldly [and] acting like mere men" (v. 3)—or as pagan unbelievers. Let's not forget that Phoebe lived just a few miles from the Corinthians and that the town she grew up in was just as pagan as Corinth.

If Phoebe could eventually become a woman who reflected God's character, so can you. God has given you all you need to grow and mature in your Christian life, no matter what your past behavior. The apostle Peter put it this way:

> His divine power has given us everything we need for life and godliness through our knowledge of him who called us by his own glory and goodness (2 Pet. 1:3).

Older Versus Younger

Since Paul emphasized the need for older women to train the younger women, you might conclude that since you are a young wife or mother or single woman, this statement by Paul doesn't apply to you. It's true that the term "older" refers to age and that the older we get, the more wisdom we hope to have to share with those younger than we are. However, when it comes to applying what Paul was teaching, there is certainly an element of relativity in this exhortation that applies at three levels.

- *First, younger Christians can teach older Christians.* Both Timothy and Titus were younger than those they were teaching, and in order to be effective, they also needed to be reverent in the way they lived (see 1 Tim. 4:12).

- *Second, we should all be an example to our peers.* Both Timothy and Titus were to be reverent in the way they lived so they could be an example to those who were basically their own age (see Titus 2:6-8).
- *Third, wisdom normally increases as we grow older.* In terms of Paul's exhortation to Titus, he recognized how important it is for older, mature women to both model and train younger women to be Christlike in all of their relationships.

Remember too that you are always older than some women in your life—younger sisters in your home, in your church and in your larger circle of friends. For example, you may be in high school. As an "older woman" you have the opportunity and responsibility to train a younger woman—say a junior high school student—to be a godly Christian. In other words, what Paul wrote to Titus about older women training younger women generally applies to all age levels.

A Tribute to a Very Special Woman

I (Gene) have received some resistance from my wife, Elaine, for including the following tribute, especially since she participated in writing this book. However, I feel this is one of those very rare occasions in our marriage when I've asked her to submit, even though she is reluctant. Anyone who knows her well also knows she is hesitant to talk about herself, whether it's in our immediate family or within the family of God in general. However, this is not Elaine speaking; it's her husband.

Elaine and I have been in the ministry together since our marriage in 1956—nearly 50 years. For 20 of these years she served with me as a professor's wife—13 years at Moody Bible Institute in Chicago and 7 years as a full-time professor at Dallas Theological

Seminary. The rest of the time has been primarily as a pastor's wife—serving alongside me in three churches where I was the founding pastor and senior leader. In all of these years, in the academic community as well as in the local church community, I have never heard one negative criticism come from her lips about either her lifestyle or her various leadership roles. The other elders and their wives with whom we have served over the years verify this observation! They have always had the highest respect for Elaine.

Is she a perfect woman—a perfect mother and perfect wife of a one-time professor and now a pastor? Not at all. Has she made mistakes? Of course. But in her humanness she has been reverent in the way she has lived! To this very day she has demonstrated that she is a woman "worthy of respect" (1 Tim. 3:11). She has a good reputation among believers and unbelievers alike.

I'm a fortunate man indeed. As many pastors and other Christian leaders will testify, they have succeeded in ministry in spite of their wives. For some, it's been an unusually difficult road. They've had to put out fires that their spouses had started. In fact, they have not been able to trust their wives with confidential information since they've known they would not keep it confidential.

I cannot think of one instance in all of our years of ministry when Elaine violated my trust with confidential information. On the other hand, I *can* remember times when I shared information with others, only to have her quickly but privately remind me that I had taken that information in confidence.

One of the authors of the book of Proverbs asked the following question: "A wife of noble character who can find?" He then continued to state that if she can be found, "She is worth far more than rubies. Her husband has full confidence in her and lacks nothing of value. She brings him good, not harm, all the days of her life" (31:10-12).

By God's grace, He enabled me to meet this kind of woman. All these years she has reflected integrity and dignity—and at times when I've made decisions that have been less than wise and prudent, she has graciously helped me get back on the right path.

Why have I written this tribute? The biblical author who described the woman of noble character in Proverbs 31 concluded his own tribute with these words—"Give her the reward she has earned" (v. 31). That is reason enough for me to pen these words about Elaine at this moment in her life. Though she knows her weaknesses—and so do I—she has exemplified Jesus Christ to me as no other human being! Thank you, Elaine! It's a privilege to write this tribute.

Though Elaine knows her weaknesses—and so do I—she has exemplified Jesus Christ to me as no other human being!

Transformed by Jesus Christ

Needless to say, no Christian woman is perfect, just as no Christian man is perfect. However, by God's grace and the power of the Holy Spirit, it's possible for Christian women (and men) to be reverent in the way they live, to live holy lives.

We must remind ourselves often that there's only been one perfect human being—the God-man, Jesus Christ. However, the Scriptures are clear that we are to imitate Christ. He is the standard by which we are to measure ourselves (see Eph. 4:13). When

Paul wrote to the Corinthians, he stated: "Follow my example, as I follow the example of Christ" (1 Cor. 11:1).

Knowing Christ Personally

Becoming like Christ must begin with a personal relationship with the Savior. The Bible calls this a born-again experience (see John 3:3). It happens as a result of faith—not works. This is why Paul wrote to the Ephesians:

> For it is by grace you have been saved, *through faith*—and this not from yourselves, it is the gift of God—not by works, so that no one can boast (2:8-9).

When we confess that we are sinners and in need of a Savior (see Rom. 3:23) and then put our faith in Jesus Christ's death and resurrection, God places us in the family of God. At that time, God's Holy Spirit comes to dwell in each of our lives enabling us to begin the journey of learning to live like Jesus Christ and to experience that "we are God's workmanship, created in Christ Jesus to do good works, which God prepared in advance for us to do" (Eph. 2:10).

Have you taken this step of faith? If not, invite the Lord Jesus Christ to be your personal Savior from sin. You can do that today—at this moment. And if you do, you'll then begin the journey of becoming more and more like Christ in all of your relationships.

A Suggested Prayer

If you are not certain of your eternal salvation, the following is a suggested prayer. Make this prayer your own heart's desire by reading the words carefully and sincerely or by formulating the thoughts into your own words.

*Dear Father in heaven, I acknowledge that I need a Savior.
I confess my sins—and I thank You that Your Son, Jesus Christ,
died on the cross to pay the penalty for my sins. I now receive the
Lord Jesus Christ as my personal Savior from sin. I believe He
died for me and rose again to give me eternal life. Thank You for
sending Your Holy Spirit to dwell in my life from this moment
forward. This I pray in Jesus' name. Amen.*

Thinking and Growing Together

The following questions are designed for group discussion after reading and studying the content of this chapter:

- Why is it important to begin our spiritual journey by making sure we have a personal salvation experience through putting our faith in Jesus Christ?
- Why is modeling so important in helping others to imitate Jesus Christ?
- Reflect on what Paul wrote about Phoebe (see Rom. 16:1-2). Why was he able to recommend her so highly?
- If someone wrote the story of your life, what would you want him or her to say about your character?
- About what can the group pray for you personally?

Set a Goal

Write out one goal you would like to achieve as a result of this study.

CHAPTER 3

Being Peacemakers

Not to be slanderers
TITUS 2:3

A Biblical Portrait of Euodia and Syntyche and Their Ongoing Conflict

These two women lived in Philippi and became very close friends. It's not known whether they were married or single, which is unimportant in their story.

The Bible does not tell when they put their faith in Jesus Christ for salvation. It's likely they may have been among the women who gathered for prayer by the river that ran through Philippi. At one of those prayer meetings, Paul shared the gospel message and Lydia and her household responded and were baptized (see Acts 16:13-15). Perhaps Euodia and Syntyche soon followed and put their faith in Jesus Christ.

It's clear from Paul's letter to the Philippians that he had a very close relationship with these two women. They had served with him in ministry. Whenever their moment of conversion, it's logical to assume that they became close friends and assisted Paul, probably on two occasions when he returned to Philippi during his third journey (Acts 20:1-6).

It's also possible that Euodia and Syntyche may have been among the official deacons that Paul greeted at the beginning of this letter—men and women who were assisting the overseers, or elders, in Philippi (see Phil. 1:1). Personally, we favor this possibility since Paul evidently used the term *diakonoi* to refer to both men and women who were involved in serving roles.[1]

An Intense Disagreement

In spite of their personal relationship with Jesus Christ and their high profile ministry in the church, tension had developed between these two women. Evidently they were still talking to each other; they just couldn't agree. Consequently, Paul addressed the problem in his letter. Note his words:

> I plead with Euodia and I plead with Syntyche to agree with each other in the Lord. Yes, and I ask you, loyal yokefellow, help these women who have contended at my side in the cause of the gospel, along with Clement and the rest of my fellow workers, whose names are in the book of life (Phil. 4:2-3).

We're not told why these two women were out of harmony with each other. If it had been a theological issue, Paul would probably have addressed it head-on as he normally did. If it had been a spiritual-life issue, he would no doubt have been as specific as he was with the Corinthians. Perhaps it was simply a personality conflict, but more than likely they couldn't agree on how to carry out the ministry in Philippi. This seems more logical, since they both seemed to be very much committed to doing God's work. After all, Paul mentioned that they both had "contended" at his side for the cause of the gospel. Here Paul used an athletic term to signify their commitment to assist Paul in communicating the gospel message. They were in the game, not on the bleachers.

A Mutual Problem

When Paul addressed this issue, he singled them out in his letter to the church at Philippi and pleaded with *both of them* "to agree with each other in the Lord." It's important to note that Paul urged each one of them, calling them by name, to take re-

We need to take responsibility for settling our differences.

sponsibility for settling their differences. In this sense, he did not put blame on either one of them but on both of them. He knew enough about the conflict to conclude it was a two-sided problem.

It's hard to imagine why Paul became so personal in a public setting. After all, this letter would have been read to the entire congregation. There seems to be at least three interrelated reasons.

First, Paul considered these women dear friends and faithful workers. Consequently, he obviously felt he could be open and honest and speak the truth in love without offending them. They knew Paul's deep appreciation for both of them and that he would never intentionally embarrass and hurt them.

Second, they apparently were very prominent leaders and may have been since the beginning of the church. This was an issue Paul felt he needed to deal with publicly. To try to settle it privately would only create rumors and would have caused other believers to take sides. The problem could have gotten much worse.

Third, it appears that the leaders in the church had already tried to solve the problem but could not. The disagreement between these two women was so intense that Epaphroditus (see Phil. 2:25-30; 4:18)—whom many believe was the church's primary overseer and pastor—couldn't resolve the issue. So when he arrived in Rome with a financial gift from the believers in Philippi, he must have shared with Paul what had happened and what continued to happen. Knowing how much these women respected Paul, with whom they served when he had ministered in Philippi, Epaphroditus probably thought, *Perhaps they will listen to Paul!*

A Leadership Challenge

This raises another interesting question: Who was the "loyal yokefellow" Paul identified as the one who could help these women resolve their problem? Though he doesn't identify this leader by name, we believe it was probably Epaphroditus—who may have penned this letter as Paul dictated. We can imagine that for a brief moment Paul looked at Epaphroditus, addressed him personally and then continued to express his thoughts to the entire church body.

Note Paul's wisdom at this moment. He not only addressed Euodia and Syntyche publicly, but he also stated before the entire congregation his confidence in Epaphroditus to be able to help these women. Apparently, neither of them had listened to this godly man—which had led to his own discouragement. If so, Paul's goal was multifaceted: to exhort these women to put aside their differences and be at peace with each other and to let them know in this public setting that he trusted Epaphroditus to solve this problem—which, of course, also let the whole church know the task Epaphroditus had ahead of him and how Paul viewed the problem. In this way, Paul solicited support from the whole Body in Philippi; he did not want people to take sides.

Paul's Personal Experience

What happened? We're never told, but since these women were true believers and sincerely dedicated to carrying out the Great Commission, we can assume they responded positively. Who knows, perhaps Paul had shared with Epaphroditus his own disagreement with Barnabas before Paul ever began the second journey, which led to the founding of the church in Philippi. The tension between Paul and Barnabas involved whether to take John Mark on the journey. In fact, their disagreement was so intense that they parted ways in carrying out the ministry (see Acts 15:39). Perhaps Paul had given Epaphroditus permission to share Paul's own story. Paul may have also been open regarding the fact that he regretted this argument and separation. After all, he and Barnabas had served together as a wonderful unified missionary team.

Paul may have also indicated how he would have done things differently if he had it to do over again so that he and Barnabas would not have gone their separate ways. Paul certainly didn't want that to happen to these two women who had contended at his side for the cause of the gospel. Furthermore, if they couldn't resolve their issues with each other, it would continue to impact the whole church. Again, it makes sense that this is why Paul would have addressed this very personal issue in such a public way. It also helps explain his earlier exhortation to the whole church to make his "joy complete by being like-minded, having the same love, being one in spirit and purpose" (Phil. 2:2).

A Woman's Reflections

In this chapter, it's a privilege to introduce you to Mary Logue, an elder's wife at Fellowship Bible Church North, who is serving with her husband, Don.

Dear Reader,

As I read this biblical portrait, I was reminded of two other ladies whom I have known for over 50 years. Their names are Clydia and Mamie. They are sisters and have never married.

These two godly women have been servants all their lives. They went to work after graduating from the eighth grade to help contribute to the family income. They have been faithful to their church, serving, singing or doing whatever is necessary. Where they differ from Euodia and Syntyche is that they are never at odds with each other. Though they are certainly human, they never seem to exhibit foolish pride or selfish ambition.

As their parents aged, Clydia and Mamie lived with them and cared for them; and now that their parents have passed away, at the ages of 91 and 87 they still live together and care for one another.

What an example and model these two ladies have been. Their lives have been dedicated to their Savior. They have not only been servants, but they have also been prayer warriors, encouragers and hard workers. To paraphrase Proverbs 31:25-26: They are women of strength and dignity and have no fear of old age. When they speak, their words are wise and kindness is the rule for everything they say. What an honor it is to know two extraordinary women like Clydia and Mamie.

As you read the rest of this chapter, think about your own relationships with other people. Has God allowed someone who is difficult to love to come into your life?

Several years ago there was a very curt and blunt person who came into my own life. She was anything but a peacemaker. Frankly, I had difficulty accepting and loving her.

Would you believe that a few months after we met, this cantankerous individual joined the same study group that I was in? Though it was not easy to interface with this lady, I soon became convinced that the Lord wanted me to deal with my own feelings. I began to pray that my heart would be changed. A short time later—much sooner than I anticipated—not only did the Lord answer my prayer, but He also gave me a love for this woman that could only have come from Him.

Perhaps you're in a similar situation as mine. Pray that your heart will be changed and that the Lord will use you to be a peacemaker.

A fellow pilgrim,
Mary Logue

The Way We Talk

Paul used a very strong word in outlining the spiritual qualification "not to be slanderers." In fact, in the New Testament the Greek word that is translated as "slanderers," *diabolos*, is also translated as "Satan" or "devil." This is understandable since Satan has been a slanderer and false accuser ever since he fell from his place of glory and honor in heaven. This is why Jesus stated that "there is no truth in him" and that "he is a liar and the father of lies" (John 8:44).

In choosing Euodia and Syntyche to illustrate the importance of this quality, we are in no way suggesting this kind of extreme behavior. However, the facts are that Satan can use even minor tension between Christians—particularly between those of us who are in leadership roles—as an opportunity to escalate the problem into a serious split among the members of the larger Body. If Satan can achieve this goal, he is thwarting what Jesus prayed for before going to the cross:

> My prayer is not for them alone [the eleven disciples]. I pray also for those who will believe in me through their message [all believers of all time], that all of them may be one, Father, just as you are in me and I am in you. May they also be in us so that the world may believe that you have sent me (John 17:20-21).

The Key to Mature Communication

James, the half brother of Christ and the primary pastoral leader in the church in Jerusalem, spoke more specifically and dramatically about the tongue and its potential for evil than did any other New Testament writer. Consider his words: "We all stumble in many ways. If anyone is never at fault in what he says, he is a perfect [or mature] man [or woman], able to keep his whole body in check" (Jas. 3:2).[2]

As stated in the previous chapter, there is only one person who lived a perfect life—the God-man, Jesus Christ. However, although nobody can ever reach perfection in this life, Jesus Christ is to be our example. How we communicate verbally serves as a precise measurement for determining our Christian maturity. If we can control our tongue, we can usually control every other part of our personality.

James used three graphic illustrations to make his point. We can control a *horse* (a large animal) by placing a *tiny bit* in his mouth. We can also direct the course of a *large ship* in all kinds of weather with a very *small rudder*. And we can set a *whole forest on fire* with a *little spark* (see Jas. 3:3-5).

This third illustration is the most dramatic—and scary. We've all seen the devastating impact of forest fires, often started by some burning embers left by a friendly camper. The tongue too is like smoldering coals. Though it is one of the smallest members of the body, it can become "a world of evil among the parts of the body. It corrupts the whole person" (Jas. 3:6). Just as a small spark can set a whole forest on fire, so the tongue can set "the whole course of [a person's] life on fire" (Jas. 3:6).

In essence, James was saying that how we use our tongue reflects on everything we do and affects everything we do. As a fire spreads through underbrush and trees of all sizes, igniting everything in its path, so a rumor, a bit of gossip or a false accusation will spread quickly and out of control. The damage can be devastating. Every tongue that repeats a rumor adds more fuel to what soon may become a raging fire.

This was Paul's concern when he urged Euodia and Syntyche to be one in spirit and purpose. Though their issues may have been minor, relatively speaking, their disagreement could have escalated into a serious conflict in the whole church because of their prominence as leaders. If that had happened, the very thing they had devoted their lives to in helping Paul, namely contending at his side for the cause of the gospel, would have been terribly marred. Their tension had the potential to even destroy their work. This, of course, was and is Satan's goal. The evil one knows that when he can destroy unity in the Church, he can destroy the effectiveness of the gospel message to those who need to hear it most.

A Fascinating Correlation

At this point, note what Paul wrote in his first letter to Timothy and in his subsequent letter to Titus. When he outlined the qualifications for the appointment of elders and overseers, Paul stated clearly that these men were to be "above reproach" (1 Tim. 3:2) and "blameless" (Titus 1:6). In both letters, Paul then followed these overarching qualities with a very specific requirement: A spiritual leader must be "the husband of but one wife" (1 Tim. 3:2; Titus 1:6), or more specifically a "man of one woman."[3] In essence, Paul was saying that the way to determine the quality of a man's reputation is to look first at his moral life.

This sequence is definitely not accidental. If a man is not loyal to one woman, his wife, he certainly cannot be trusted to lead a church. Men who commit adultery and who are unrepentant will also lie and be deceptive in other matters. Frankly, we have never seen an exception to this reality in all our years of ministry together.

But note another observation as it relates to Paul's statements about women who are in leadership roles (see figure 1). In the same section of Paul's letter to Timothy, Paul outlined the character qualities for women who serve in the church as deacons.[4] They were "to be women worthy of respect" (1 Tim. 3:11). Then in the same verse Paul followed this overarching quality with the requirement that these women not be "malicious talkers."

Note the same basic pattern in his letter to Titus (again see figure 1). Older women who are qualified to train younger women are to be "reverent in the way they live" (Titus 2:3). And in the same verse, Paul followed this overarching quality with the injunction that they are "not to be slanderers" (Titus 2:3).

FIGURE 1

A COMPARISON OF QUALIFICATIONS FOR MALE ELDERS AND FEMALE LEADERS

Male Elders	Female Leaders
In 1 Timothy: "Above reproach" (3:2) "The husband of but one wife" (3:2)	In 1 Timothy (deacons): "Worthy of respect" (3:11) "Not malicious talkers" (3:11)
In Titus: "Blameless" (1:6) "The husband of but one wife" (1:6)	In Titus (older women): "Reverent in the way they live" (2:3) "Not to be slanderers" (2:3)

What was Paul saying about the differences between men and women and how these variations can affect our reputation? Clearly, a man's major temptation and weakness is *sexual* (to be immoral). Stated positively, moral purity does more to build a man's reputation than do all the qualities that follow on Paul's list. On the other hand, a woman's major temptation and weakness is *verbal* (to communicate in ways that are destructive). Stated positively, a woman who controls her tongue and is a peacemaker does more to build her reputation than having all the other qualities Paul listed. This, of course, does *not* mean that both men and women are not tempted in both areas. What it *does* mean, however, is that, based on gender, these are areas of vulnerability and weakness that can also become areas of strength and thus build men's and women's reputations.

A Charge to All Believers

When Paul appealed to Christ's example earlier in his letter to the Philippians (see 2:5-8), he was setting the stage for his specific exhortation to Euodia and Syntyche. Jesus Christ, who was equal with God, became human and demonstrated the greatest act of humility known in the universe—death on a cross. He who was God in human flesh stooped and washed the feet of His disciples, men who had been *arguing among themselves* who was to be the greatest in God's kingdom (see John 13:2-17; Luke 22:24-30).

Paul wrote that if we are to follow Christ's example, we should "do nothing out of selfish ambition or vain conceit, but in humility consider others better than [ourselves]. [We] should look not only to [our] own interests, but also to the interests of others" (Phil. 2:3-4).

To become this kind of Christian, all of us as believers must be careful in what we say. James said it best:

> Everyone should be quick to listen, slow to speak and slow to become angry (Jas. 1:19).

A Final Word

When Paul stated that women who are in training roles should not be slanderers, he was, of course, dealing first and foremost with malicious gossip. This is also what James described in his letter. Gossip is deliberately hurtful. It is based on envy and rooted in flagrant selfishness. It is designed to break up relationships and destroy friendships.

For most of us, however, there is a far more subtle danger of gossip: the tendency to rationalize our gossip. It's so dangerous because it's based on self-deception. We deceive ourselves into believing that we are sharing information for the good of the other person. We may disguise it by calling it a prayer interest or a personal concern. Nevertheless, this kind of communication can become very destructive.

Another common type of gossip may be classified as inadvertent. In fact, this kind of communication may actually be motivated by our desire to be helpful. But in reality, we may also be trying to prove to others *how helpful we really are.* For example, we've known women who love to share prayer requests about others, but it's obvious to most people that these women are experiencing emotional gratification from talking about others in this way. In these situations, there is a very fine line between pure motives and impure motives. The Scriptures make it clear that whatever we say should be to build others up, not to hurt them. It's better to be safe than sorry.

Thinking and Growing Together

The following questions are designed for group discussion after reading and studying the content of this chapter:

- Share a personal experience in which you've seen innocent comments mushroom into malicious gossip. What happened?
- How can we avoid hurting others—even with prayer requests?
- Why is this requirement that older women who are training younger women not be slanderers so important?
- How does Paul's requirement in his letter to Titus relate to husband-and-wife relationships? To family relationships?
- About what can the group pray for you personally?

Set a Goal

Write out one goal you would like to achieve as a result of this discussion.

Finding Freedom in Christ

[Not to be] addicted to much wine
TITUS 2:3

A Biblical Portrait of Mary Magdalene, a Woman Set Free

There are at least six significant women named Mary who are mentioned in the New Testament. Jesus' mother, of course, stands out as the most well known in religious history. But there is another that grabs the attention of anyone who is interested in the way in which the gospel can transform a person's life. She is often identified as Mary Magdalene.

This Mary probably was born and grew up in a small village called Magdala on the western shore of the Sea of Galilee. Just five miles north and slightly to the east in Capernaum, a prosperous fishing town, Jesus had set up His home base for His Galilean ministry.

Freedom from Demon Possession

During one of His many journeys along the Galilean seashore, Mary encountered Jesus. We're not told how she behaved during that initial meeting. We can only assume that her actions were far from normal since she and several other women were demon possessed. They heard Jesus "proclaiming the good news of the kingdom of God" (Luke 8:1). As Luke listed these women, he mentioned Mary Magdalene first. Perhaps she was the most troubled—since Jesus had to cast seven demons out of her. Incredibly grateful, Mary and the other women who had experienced this new freedom began to follow Jesus and the apostles and supported them with their own financial resources (see Luke 8:2-3).

A Perpetuated Myth

Though the city of Magdala had a negative reputation because of immorality, there is no evidence that Mary was a prostitute. This is a myth that has been perpetuated over the centuries.

Commitment to Jesus

Though several other women are mentioned by name in the final weeks of Jesus' life on Earth, Mary Magdalene takes center stage. As she looked up at the cross as Jesus shed His blood for the sins of the world, her pain must have been unbearable (see Matt. 27:55-56). In the Louvre in Paris hangs a painting that portrays

Mary Magdalene that terrible night of the crucifixion. Regarding this classic painting, someone commented,

> The world is wrapped in shadow, the stars are dead; and yet in the darkness is seen a kneeling form. It is Mary Magdalene with loving lips and hands pressing against the bleeding feet of Christ.[1]

With overwhelming sadness, Mary Magdalene watched and followed Joseph and Nicodemus as they took Christ's body down from the cross and laid it in a new tomb (see John 19:38-42; Mark 15:47). Then, on the first day of the week as dawn appeared in the eastern sky, Mary boldly led the way to the tomb to anoint Jesus' body with spices (see Mark 16:1). Discovering that the grave was empty and believing Jesus' body had been stolen, she quickly ran and reported this alarming news to Peter and John (see John 20:1-2). But perhaps the most significant fact about Mary Magdalene is that she was the first person on Earth to see Jesus alive and to report this good news to the disciples (see John 20:18). What an incredible honor!

In all of these events, except for the resurrection scene, other women participated. However, Mary Magdalene's name is always mentioned first, indicating her prominence in the biblical story. She more than all the others was probably the most active in following her Savior and caring for His earthly needs. After all, she at one time was possessed by seven demons. We can only imagine the depth of her bondage and how grateful she was when they no longer had control of her life.

A Woman's Reflections

It's a privilege to introduce you to Linda Cole, another elder's wife at Fellowship Bible Church North. She serves with her husband, Jack.

Dear Reader,

As I reflect on these words about Mary Magdalene, I am moved by her deep devotion to Jesus Christ. Her desire to be in His presence and to serve Him was her response to His gracious gift of healing and freedom. Her life and commitment spurs me on to be aware of all that Christ has done for me so that I too may experience His presence moment by moment and joyfully serve Him by allowing Him to serve others through me.

You may wonder how this chapter on not being addicted to much wine has personal relevance if drinking has not been a problem for you. This has not been one of my weaknesses either. In fact, I used to be very prideful and self-righteous about the fact that I didn't have this particular addiction.

However, I've since learned that addictions can come in many forms. My addictions just happened to be more socially acceptable: chocolate, caffeine, busyness and the need to please others.

Please don't misunderstand. There's nothing wrong with any of these things in and of themselves. However, if I'm using them to cope with the pressures of my life instead of turning to Christ, then I am in bondage—and that bondage is just as addictive and sinful as the ones I consider socially unacceptable.

Christ came to set me free, and I am learning how to depend on Him and Him alone to meet every need in my life so that I will not be addicted to anything. I'm free to choose many things, but I also can choose to abstain from anything that might cause another to stumble. The freedom we have been given in Christ is indeed a very great gift.

As you read the rest of this chapter, think about the freedom you have in Christ. But also, remember the words of Paul to the Galatians:

You, my brothers [and sisters], were called to be free. But do not use your freedom to indulge the sinful nature [or the flesh]; rather, serve one another in love (Gal. 5:13).

Yours because of His love,
Linda Cole

Addictive Behaviors

You may wonder why we have chosen Mary Magdalene to set the stage for a discussion on the character quality of not being addicted to much wine. There's one major reason: Mary Magdalene's problems could very well have encompassed every addiction you can name, including alcohol. Though there is no evidence that she was a prostitute, we can only imagine the sexual sins associated with her demon possession. But Jesus Christ set her free from all of her addictions. She was no longer in bondage to forces beyond her control.

It's not our intention in this chapter to discuss demon possession and its impact on people today. We know it was prevalent in Jesus' day and we also know it exists today. But we're also quite convinced that what are often classified as the demons of alcohol, tobacco and various kinds of drugs are in reality obsessions and compulsions that are related to various personalities and to the substances themselves. There is plenty of medical evidence, for example, that alcoholism is not only a spiritual disease, but a psychological and physiological sickness as well. Consequently, it must be treated both spiritually and medically.

Is Satan at the root of these problems? You can be sure he is! When he deceived Eve in the Garden of Eden and she succumbed, Satan set in motion a spiritual sickness that has affected each of us, even to this day—a sickness that includes the body, soul and spirit. It's called sin, and unless we experience personal redemption and salvation, it separates us from God. Furthermore, all sin puts us in bondage to certain fleshly appetites until we are set free in Jesus Christ (see Gal. 5:1).

First-Century Intemperance

In the Roman world, drinking wine was as common as consuming soft drinks in our culture. And even though wine was not as strong in alcoholic content as our wines are today, it was possible to become addicted. It was simply a matter of intake.

In those days in the Roman Empire, many women probably used wine as a means to alleviate the emotional pain of having to fulfill the role expected of a woman. Who wouldn't want to forget the problems of just being a slave, a convenience, a bearer of children in order to enhance a man's reputation in the community. Gentile women who had no hope beyond this life would be especially susceptible. As Paul said to the Ephesians, "Remember that at that time you were separate from Christ, excluded from citizenship in Israel and foreigners to the covenants of the promise, *without hope* and *without God* in the world" (2:12).

But Jesus Christ changed all that. Knowing the Savior gave men and women eternal hope. He also gave women a new goal in this life. Spiritually, women were elevated to a position of equality with men. As Paul wrote to the Galatians, "There is neither Jew nor Greek, slave nor free, *male nor female* . . . in Christ Jesus." We "are all one" (Gal. 3:28). And Peter exhorted men to treat their wives as "heirs"—heirs "of the gracious gift of life" (1 Pet. 3:7).

Paul, of course, put it very straight and heavy when he told husbands they were to love their wives "just as Christ loved the church" (Eph. 5:25). What a new experience! This meant no more physical and psychological abuse! No more sex with women other than their wives! In Christ, there was to be a brand-new relationship. This, of course, changed a woman's whole environment, and in changing her environment, it changed her life.

But old habits are difficult to break. Emotional and psychological hurt doesn't disappear overnight. It took time for some of these New Testament women to develop Christian maturity in all aspects of their lives. And, of course, it took time for men to love their wives as Christ loved them. Imagine their struggle to overcome their own addictions—especially those that were sexual in nature. And lack of control in the area of drinking wine was a persistent temptation for both men and women, particularly for those who had become addicted.

A True Biblical Perspective

This leads to a very practical question. Does the Bible teach total abstinence? Paul instructed both Timothy and Titus to never choose elders to oversee the church who were "*addicted* to wine" (1 Tim. 3:3, *NASB*; Titus 1:7, *NASB*), but he did not say never to choose elders who ever *drank* wine. And rest assured that Paul was not referring to grape juice, since it's impossible to be addicted to grape juice. He was definitely talking about an alcoholic beverage.

We cannot make the Bible teach that it is always wrong to drink alcoholic beverages. But when we have a total biblical perspective, we may decide on total abstinence, particularly in our culture. But what does the Bible teach?

Drunkenness

Overdrinking is out of the will of God.

The Bible clearly teaches against drunkenness. This is true in both the Old Testament and the New Testament. In Proverbs we read,

Do not join those who drink too much wine or gorge themselves on meat, for drunkards and gluttons become poor, and drowsiness clothes them in rags (23:20-21).

Later in the same chapter, we discover a series of questions: "Who has woe? Who has sorrow? Who has strife? Who has complaints? Who has needless bruises? Who has bloodshot eyes?" (v. 29). We then find the answer to all of them: "Those who linger long over wine, who go to sample bowls of mixed wine" (v. 30).

Finally, following this explicit paragraph on the price people pay when they indulge, we discover a serious warning:

Do not gaze at wine when it is red, when it sparkles in the cup, when it goes down smoothly! In the end it bites like a snake and poisons like a viper. Your eyes will see strange sights and your mind imagine confusing things (vv. 31-33).

The New Testament writers are just as clear in their teaching against overdrinking that leads to drunkenness. Paul wrote to the Ephesians,

Do not get drunk on wine, which leads to debauchery. Instead, be filled with the Spirit (5:18).

Addictions

Drinking alcoholic beverages is out of God's will when we are addicted.

In 1 Corinthians 6:12, Paul warned against addiction, and in his letters to Timothy and Titus, addiction to alcohol was Paul's primary concern. Unfortunately, America has the same need to heed Paul's warnings because our society is permeated with alcoholics.

Being a Stumbling Block

Drinking alcoholic beverages is out of the will of God when it causes others to sin.

The Bible teaches that we should not cause others to stumble and fall into sin. Paul wrote to the Romans,

It is better not to eat meat or drink wine or to do anything else that will cause your brother [or sister] to fall (14:21).

It's common knowledge that children of alcoholics run a much greater risk of becoming alcoholics than do children of nonalcoholics. True, we can engage in the age-old argument regarding what causes alcoholism—heredity or the environment. We believe both are involved. Some people are born with a propensity for alcoholism, but it is also true that *modeling plays a great part in causing them to start drinking in the first place.*

Harming Our Bodies

Drinking alcoholic beverages is out of the will of God when we hurt others or ourselves.

If we are Christians, our bodies are temples of the Holy Spirit. He dwells within us. Therefore we are not to harm ourselves. We are not our own. We are bought with a price. "Therefore glorify God in your body" (1 Cor. 6:20, *NASB*).

Lack of Moderation

Overindulging in anything is out of the will of God.

As we look at what the Scriptures teach about alcohol, we must not overlook the fact that it also teaches that we must never overindulge in anything. For example, notice how often *eating* and

For some people total abstinence is the better way to live.

drinking are mentioned together in the Bible (see Deut. 21:20, *NASB*; Prov. 23:21; Matt. 11:19; Luke 7:34). There are Christians who overeat regularly but would never touch a drop of alcohol. Unfortunately, some of these Christians are the most vociferous in judging others who drink socially. Yet they are consistently overweight, not because of glandular problems, but because of a lack of self-discipline. Jesus Christ had some strong words to say to these Christians:

Why do you look at the speck of sawdust in your brother's eye and pay no attention to the plank in your own eye? How can you say to your brother, "Let me take the speck out of your eye," when all the time there is a plank in your own eye? You hypocrite, first take the plank out of your own eye, and then you will see clearly to remove the speck from your brother's eye (Matt. 7:3-5).

A Higher Principle

Although Paul did not teach total abstinence and although he instructed Timothy to "use a little wine" (1 Tim. 5:23) for health reasons, he also told the Romans, "It is better not to eat meat or drink wine or to do anything else that will cause your brother to fall" (14:21). The issue Paul was concerned about in Romans 14 was not the meat or the wine per se; rather, it was the idolatrous associations and the problems that partaking may have created for weak Christians. Paul was saying that for some people total abstinence is the better way to live. *Love and concern for others is the higher principle,* and a mature, sensitive Christian is willing to avoid certain activities, although the activities may be legitimate in themselves. Does anything in your life violate this broader and higher principle? This is a very important question for older women—challenged by the apostle Paul to train younger women to be godly—to ask themselves.

Questions to Evaluate Your Personal Lifestyle

Now, consider the following questions in order to evaluate your lifestyle:

- Am I still controlled by any habits that were part of my non-Christian lifestyle? Intemperance usually involves a lack of self-control.
  __ overeating
  __ overspending
  __ oversleeping
  __ overworking
  __ overindulging in anything!
- What are my motives for doing what I do?
  __ Some people overeat when they are under stress.
  __ Some people chain-smoke because they're nervous.
  __ Some people overdrink because they're anxious.
  __ Some people overspend on clothes and items for the home because they feel inferior and insecure.

__ Some people travel a great deal to run away from personal problems and basic responsibilities.

Can I list other reasons why people are excessive in the things they do?

• Are my problems *psychological* or purely *habitual*?

There's a very fine line between these two causes. However, there is usually a distinction. People who have psychological causes for intemperance usually operate at an obsessive level and their behavior doesn't really make sense to them. Additionally, the very thought of change can be threatening and can cause even more anxiety.

Thinking and Growing Together

The following questions are designed for group discussion after reading and studying the content of this chapter:

• Why are there so many addictive behaviors in our culture?
• Why is it so important that people who teach others be free from addictive behaviors?
• Why is it important to have an accountability group in overcoming addictions?
• When it comes to addictions, why should Christians take James's instruction to seek prayer from local church elders seriously (see Jas. 5:13-16)?
• About what can the group pray for you personally?

Set a Goal

Write out one goal you would like to achieve as a result of this discussion.

CHAPTER 5

Communicating Godliness

To teach what is good

TITUS 2:3

A Biblical Portrait of Priscilla, a Gifted Teacher

When it comes to teaching what is good, a woman named Priscilla quickly emerges in the New Testament story. Though she's always mentioned along with her husband, Aquila, she was definitely "an older woman" who had a unique teaching ministry. This husband and wife team first appears in the book of Acts, but note Paul's greeting and tribute several years later in his letter to the Romans:

> Greet Priscilla and Aquila, my fellow workers in Christ Jesus. They risked their lives for me. Not only I but all the churches of the Gentiles are grateful to them (Rom. 16:3-4).

Priscilla's Unique Position

It's not an accident that Priscilla's name appears first in this greeting and commendation. Name order is very significant in the New Testament; it indicates prominence. And as we unfold what we know about Priscilla, it's clear that she stands out in this husband-wife relationship as having a unique teaching ministry.

We mustn't conclude, however, that Priscilla was the leader in her home. Luke seemed to make that apparent in his first reference to this couple when he introduced us to "Aquila, a native of Pontus, who had recently come from Italy with his wife Priscilla" (Acts 18:2). Prior to his becoming a believer, he was probably a typical Jewish husband in terms of the way he viewed his patriarchal leadership role in the family. But when he became a follower of Jesus Christ through Paul's influence, he recognized his wife's giftedness and ability to assist in carrying out the Great Commission. In fact, Aquila was evidently not concerned or threatened when his wife at times took the lead in providing guidance for people—both men and women—who needed spiritual help.

Anti-Semitism

Let's unfold their story. Aquila and Priscilla had been forced to leave Rome when Emperor Claudius issued an order that all the Jews were to leave the city (see Acts 18:2). Like so many Gentile leaders in world history, Claudius was definitely anti-Semitic. Traveling to Corinth, this couple established a tentmaking business. Since Paul had learned the same trade growing up in Tarsus, he joined Aquila and Priscilla in their business venture and spent weekends sharing the gospel in the local synagogue (see Acts 18:3-4).

Conversion to Jesus Christ

Apparently this husband and wife became believers while in Corinth. We can certainly conclude that they probably had many opportunities to listen to their business partner and friend explain and interpret the Old Testament prophecies regarding Jesus Christ. Since Paul regularly went into the synagogues to reason with the people, it's logical to assume that Aquila and Priscilla were a part of those discussions. From what we know about Priscilla, she probably asked some of the toughest questions.

Once they received Jesus Christ as their Messiah, they became so committed to Paul's ministry that when he left Corinth, they accompanied him until they reached Ephesus (see Acts 18:19). Maturing in their faith, they stayed on in Ephesus to continue to witness to their fellow Jews while Paul went on to his home church in Antioch (see Acts 18:21-22,24-26).

Back to Rome

Eventually the ban on Jews living in Rome was lifted, so this dedicated couple left Ephesus and went back to their home in the Imperial City. It was there that Paul identified this couple in his letter to the Romans as his "fellow workers in Christ Jesus" who had "risked their lives" for him (16:3-4). Obviously they loved Jesus Christ, they loved Paul, and they loved the work of God. And when Paul greeted them following their return to Rome, they once again opened their home as a meeting place for Christians (see v. 5).

A Theological Lesson

In terms of Priscilla's ability "to teach what is good" (Titus 2:3), Luke recorded in Acts 18:24-26 a very significant event that happened in Ephesus after Paul left Ephesus and returned to Antioch. Apollos, a very astute and educated Jew, arrived in Ephesus. He was well informed regarding the Old Testament and believed that Jesus was indeed the promised Messiah. Like Paul, Apollos spoke "boldly in the synagogue" (v. 26). However, he didn't have a complete knowledge of the gospel message. In some respects, his understanding stopped with his knowledge of John's baptism. Having learned the rest of the story from the apostle Paul, "*Priscilla* and *Aquila* . . . invited him to their home and explained to him the way of God more adequately" (v. 26).

It seems that Priscilla took the lead both in evaluating what Apollos was teaching and in inviting him to their home. In fact, she may have also taken the lead in filling in the gaps in his knowledge: that the Holy Spirit baptizes all true believers into the Body of Jesus Christ (see 1 Cor. 12:13) and that water baptism following this conversion experience symbolizes the death, burial and resurrection of Jesus Christ (see Matt. 28:19-20; Rom. 6:1-4). Regardless, Luke made it very clear that both Priscilla and Aquila (in that order) were involved in explaining "the way of God more adequately" (Acts 18:26). Again, remember that name order is very important in Scripture in signifying prominence in various situations.[1]

This, of course, is only one instance of many in which Aquila and Priscilla served together as a dedicated team. In fact, Paul mentioned in his letter to the Romans that "*all the churches* of the Gentiles are grateful to them" (16:4). They were Paul's fellow workers, and they actually put their lives in danger in order to protect their dear friend and fellow minister.

A Woman's Reflections

It's a privilege to introduce you to Shannon Hansen, who serves along with her husband, Dirk, an elder at Fellowship Bible Church North.

Dear Reader,

As I read the biblical portrait of Priscilla, as well as the rest of this chapter, I was reminded of a similar situation in my own life when I had the opportunity to teach what is good. I was leading 12 women in a Bible study on a mother's role. During one of our discussions, we began talking about the deity of Christ. I pointed to the Scriptures that teach that Jesus is the Son of God and that He and the Father are one.

We then took a break, and as we were walking down the hall to get our coffee, one of the young mothers in our group approached me with some apprehension. "Shannon," she said as she touched my arm, "I'm confused. You said that Jesus is God. Do you really believe that?"

I asked her about her background and she told me that her husband was a Jehovah's Witness, and although she didn't totally embrace his views, she really didn't know what to believe. Sensing I needed more time to explore her question in a private setting, I asked her if she would like to meet with me one-on-one. She agreed, and together we looked up Scripture references about Jesus, His deity and His claims to be one with the Father.

Three weeks later this sincere seeker prayed to receive the Lord Jesus Christ as her personal Savior. We then began praying for her husband! Because my friend lived a godly life in front of her husband, he too eventually believed that Jesus Christ was indeed one with the Father and was the Son of God, and he put his faith in the Lord Jesus Christ for salvation.

I praise the Lord for giving me the opportunity to teach this woman what is good. Let me encourage you to seize every opportunity to teach what is good to those around you. I could have easily told this woman that she needed to talk to our pastor or just give her Scriptures to look up on her own. I'm thankful that the Holy Spirit had other ideas and gave me courage and a desire to spend time with her personally.

Frankly, I was nervous. What if she asked me something I didn't know? But God is faithful, and He gave me the truths she needed to hear. He will do the same for you. I pray that what you're about to read will challenge you to be available to others who need your help.

Yours sincerely,
Shannon Hansen

Communicating God's Character

The phrase "to teach what is good" actually comes from one Greek word (*kalodidaskalos*). *Didaskalos* means "teacher" and *kalos* refers to something that is morally good, noble, praiseworthy and blameless. In fact, Paul used "kalos," translated as "good," a few sentences later when he exhorted Titus regarding his ministry to young men:

> Similarly, encourage the young men to be self-controlled. In everything set them an example by *doing what is good* [kalos]. In your *teaching* show *integrity, seriousness* and *soundness of speech* that cannot be condemned (Titus 2:6-8).

Modeling Biblical Truth

This passage clearly explains what Paul meant when he instructed Titus to "teach the older women . . . to *teach what is good*" (2:3).

Note again that Paul's focus in verse 7 is primarily on being an example to the young men. Before Titus could effectively *teach* what is *good*, he was to *do* what is *good*. This is the same message he was to convey to the older women in Crete. They were to be reverent in the way they lived so that they could effectively train the younger women how to live the Christian life in all of their relationships (vv. 4-5).

As we stated in chapter 2, modeling is a foundational concept in New Testament communication. In order to help older women grasp this two-dimensional teaching-and-training process, Titus was to exemplify this quality in his own teaching. In his life he was to practice with the younger men what he was also teaching the older women to do with the younger women.

Three Characteristics

To build a model for effective teaching, Paul listed three attributes: Titus was to practice what he taught—to show *integrity* in his teaching; he was to earn the privilege of being heard by communicating with *seriousness*; and the content of his teaching was to reflect *soundness of speech*—to be carefully and accurately presented. Otherwise, those who were in opposition to Christ and the "trustworthy message" (Titus 1:9) would be able to attack Titus's character and hurt the cause of Christ. However, if Titus set an example by doing what is good—in every thing and in every way—his opposition would be put to shame and would ultimately be silenced.

Again, this is an elaboration on what Paul had in mind for older women who were to train younger women. In exhorting Titus to be an example as he taught younger men, Paul was explaining what he meant when he wrote that older women were to teach what is good to younger women.

A Task for Older Women

Note at this point that Paul did not exhort Titus to teach the younger women—at least in the specific areas he outlined, which we'll look at carefully in the next chapters. Rather, Titus was to equip the older women to carry out this task. This does not mean that Titus wasn't to teach all age groups "what is in accord with sound doctrine" (2:1). But when it came to guiding the younger women in the rather personal and intimate issues regarding their relationships with their husbands and children, he was to teach the older women to fulfill this responsibility. The reasons are obvious.

First, godly older women can communicate with younger women in ways that men cannot. These are women-to-women issues. Being a man, Titus could not identify experientially with these issues.

Second, Titus was a relatively young man who was probably single. Paul wanted to ensure that Titus would not create a vulnerable situation for either himself or the young women in these local churches. We see Paul's same concern for Timothy when he was ministering in Ephesus. He was to "treat younger men as *brothers,* older women as *mothers,* and younger women as *sisters,* with *absolute purity*" (1 Tim. 5:1-2).

Godless Myths and Old Wives' Tales

In Paul's first letter to Timothy, he added further clarification to teaching what is good by contrasting it with teachings that are *not* good. Paul warned that there will be those—particularly as Christianity unfolds—who "will abandon the faith and follow deceiving spirits and things taught by demons" (1 Tim. 4:1). Becoming very specific, Paul stated that "such teachings come through hypocritical liars, whose consciences have been seared as with a hot iron" (v. 2). These people will have distorted views regarding marriage and family life—even teaching that those who do not marry are more holy than those who do. They will also teach people to "abstain from certain foods, which God created to be received with thanksgiving by those who believe and who know the truth" (v. 3).

Paul then culminated this thought with the following words of encouragement to Timothy:

> If you point these things out to the brothers [and sisters], you will be a *good minister* of Christ Jesus, brought up in the *truths of the faith* and of the *good teaching* that you have followed. Have nothing to do with *godless myths and old wives' tales;* rather, train yourself to be godly (vv. 6-7).

Paul's point is clear, and it applies in a very unique but direct way to his instructions to Titus regarding women teaching women. To teach what is *good,* to be a *good* minister, to be involved in *good* teaching, means communicating what is true, what is from God and what is God's will. In short, it means teaching the Word of God, not false doctrine that is based on myths and old wives' tales.

A Personal Experience

We vividly remember a situation in our own women's ministry. An older woman had been asked to teach the Bible to a group of younger women. Before long we got feedback that all was not well. The teacher had become enamored with a man's teaching who claimed to be a prophet and to have received special messages from God as to when Jesus was going to return and who the Antichrist was going to be. Unfortunately, this woman began communicating this message to the younger women in the Bible study. A few actually believed what was being taught! Some became confused, but others knew this was false teaching. As you can imagine, it became a very sensitive and tense situation.

As things began to deteriorate, one of our pastors stepped in to fill a Timothy and Titus role, namely to be "a *good minister* of Christ Jesus" (1 Tim. 4:6). In a very mature and sensitive way, he brought theological clarity to the situation; and the teacher, rather than correcting her views, eventually resigned. Though we had to do damage control, the fallout was minimal compared with what it would have been if the pastor had not addressed this false teaching head-on. It could have become devastating to many of our young women—and potentially to the whole church.

Incidentally, the false prophet who was at the root of the problem soon passed from the scene and into obscurity. The dates he had set for Christ's return passed by—as they always have and always will—since as Jesus said, no one knows the day or the hour of His return (see Matt. 24:36). Furthermore, the man who was prophesied to be the Antichrist is still alive but is obviously not the "man of lawlessness" (2 Thess. 2:3) whom Paul described in his second letter to the Thessalonians (see vv. 1-3).

The Most Important Lesson

We learned some significant lessons from this experience. Most important, we had not evaluated this older woman's personal history and character sufficiently to place her in such a strategic position. Furthermore, we had not evaluated her ideas regarding how to study the Scriptures. For example, she believed and taught that all any one person needs to interpret the Scriptures accurately is a Bible and the Holy Spirit. In other words, every individual Christian can be a loner in Bible exploration.

Though all of us are certainly encouraged to study the Scriptures on our own, loner Bible exploration ultimately becomes a very dangerous philosophy if we negate the importance of interacting with others regarding our observations and conclusions. This approach to Bible study violates the need for all Christians to study the Scriptures in community. This is why the Body of Christ is so important. All of us, regardless of our background and experience, are capable of subjectively interpreting the Word of God, which can lead to theological error. It's only "as each part does its work" within the Body of Christ that it "grows and builds itself up in love" (Eph. 4:16). This applies to all aspects of spiritual growth, including Bible study.

To be able to teach, we must be able to communicate with others in a nonthreatening, nondefensive and teachable manner.

Able to Teach

When Paul wrote his final letter to Timothy, he used the term *didaktikos* to describe a certain kind of teaching. In English, translators use the phrases "able to teach" or "apt to teach" to describe what Paul meant. Timothy was to look for this quality in men who were to be appointed as elders (see 1 Tim. 3:2). But in his second letter, Paul explained what this kind of teaching should look like in Timothy's own ministry:

> Don't have anything to do with foolish and stupid arguments, because you know they produce quarrels. And the Lord's servant must not quarrel; instead, he must be

kind to everyone, *able to teach,* not resentful. Those who oppose him he must gently instruct, in the hope that God will grant them repentance leading them to a knowledge of the truth (2 Tim. 2:23-25).

When we see this concept in context, it's clear that "didaktikos" (able to teach) has a far broader meaning than just pedagogical methodology. Dr. Phil Williams, a good friend of ours through the years and a professor of Greek who now is with the Lord, believed that this word could be translated as "teachable" because of its root meaning and its use in classical Greek. We certainly respect Phil's opinion because he studied both classical Greek and Koine Greek, the original language of the New Testament. We believe, however, that "didaktikos" has a far more profound meaning: the ability to communicate in a humble, sensitive, nondefensive and, yes, teachable way. You see, the meaning of "didaktikos" in classical Greek, which predated New Testament Greek, did mean "teachable." However, by the time Paul used the word "didaktikos," its meaning had evolved to incorporate both the concept of teachability as well as a person's spiritual and psychological maturity in communicating truth to others—especially to those who may disagree with the message of Scripture.

This is not surprising, since the meanings of words in all languages change over time. Usually, however, these words contain elements of meaning from the past. For example, when the *King James Version* of the Bible was translated, the word "conversation" referred to our manner of life, our total lifestyle. However, in modern English the word "conversation" means our verbal communication, not the way we live our lives in a complete sense. (Compare Phil. 1:27 in the original *King James Version* with the same verse in the *New King James Version;* what the *King James Version* translates as "conversation," the *New King James Version* translates as "conduct.")

In terms of "didaktikos," we can clearly see this process of change in meaning when we look at the passage from 2 Timothy 2 that we just quoted. Note that the English words "able to teach" are surrounded by a cluster of words that describe qualities of life, not skills. In his communication, Timothy was to be *nonargumentative*. He was to be *kind* to all people, Christians and non-Christians. He was to be *patient* even when he was falsely accused and personally attacked. He was to correct in a *gentle* manner those who were opposing him. And note that sandwiched right in the middle of these qualities of life is the word "didaktikos," translated as "able to teach."

What does this mean practically? To demonstrate being able to teach, we must possess certain personal qualities that enable us to communicate with others in a nonthreatening, nondefensive and teachable manner ourselves. We must not be the kind of people who go around looking for arguments or stirring them up. We must be sensitive to people, including those who are confused, obstinate or bitter. When verbally abused, we must not reciprocate with cutting words and putdowns. In short, men and women who are able to teach are people who are not in bondage to themselves. They're secure as individuals, and they're in control of their minds and emotions.

An Embarassing Story

I (Gene) remember one time when, as a young Bible institute teacher, I did not demonstrate well this quality of being able to teach. A man who was several years older than I was kept disagreeing with me in class session after class session. One day I became so infuriated with his behavior that I gathered up my lecture notes, dismissed the class and walked out the door, leaving the students to fend for themselves.

Later, this man came to my office to apologize and ask for forgiveness. It was then that I learned why he had tried so hard to intimidate and irritate me. You see, as a young single professor, I began dating a girl on campus, who is now my wife. There were no rules against a professor dating a student, but so as not to create any problems, we kept our courtship private, seeing each other off campus. However, when Elaine suddenly began wearing an engagement ring, it became an instant topic of conversation throughout the student body. It was a complete surprise to almost everyone. In my office that day, this man confessed that he had had his eye on the same girl and was trying to generate courage to ask her out. Unknown to him, I was already in a dating relationship with Elaine. In his mind, I had beaten him to the draw. I, of course, was completely unaware of his intentions and feelings. Once he unraveled his story, it all made sense.

In retrospect, had I been more mature, I could have handled the situation in a much better way. If I had it to do over again, I would have asked this student to see me after class to discuss his concerns. I probably would have found out the reason for his attitudes and actions. Furthermore, I would have demonstrated more Christlikeness to the students—that I was really able to teach, in the full sense of what that means.

I've never forgotten that experience. It taught me a great lesson. I hope that in similar circumstances, I have handled these situations in a much more godly fashion. My experience reveals that all of us become more mature in our Christian lives through actual hands-on experience. Some of our greatest spiritual lessons can come from our failures.

Thinking and Growing Together

The following questions are designed for group discussion after reading and studying the content of this chapter:

- How do you see the principle of studying the Scriptures in community illustrated in the lives of Priscilla and Aquila?
- What happens when Bible teachers do not model the biblical truth they are attempting to communicate? Without being critical or judgmental, can you share some personal observations?
- What experiences have you had in which someone distorted the teachings of Scripture? Why did this happen? What resulted?
- How does the quality of being able to teach, as described and illustrated in this chapter, apply to parents and children?
- About what can the group pray for you personally?

Set a Goal

Write out one goal you would like to achieve as a result of this discussion.

CHAPTER 6

Loving Your Husband

To love their husbands

TITUS 2:4

A Biblical Portrait of Naomi, a Mentor in the Midst of Tragedy

To illustrate the quality of loving your husband, let's go back to a dynamic Old Testament story. We're referring to Ruth, the Moabitess. Many consider this the most idyllic love story in the

Bible. However, in our vignette, our focus is not on Ruth per se but on her mother-in-law, Naomi.

These events took place during the rule of judges in Israel— when "everyone did as he saw fit" (Judg. 21:25). Naomi, her husband, Elimelech, and their family lived in Bethlehem and were affected by a serious famine. This famine probably happened because of Israel's sinful behavior; God had told them that He would judge His people in this way if they turned to false gods (see Deut. 28:14-24).

Walking Out of God's Will

To survive, Elimelech decided to leave the land of Judah and travel to Moab, which was situated east of the Dead Sea. There they lived in a pagan culture. Though it was only 30 miles southeast of Bethlehem, it was a great distance in terms of their relationship with God. They were able to meet their physical needs, but they faced a spiritual famine. Since as a family they were not walking in the will of God, they may have not even recognized how spiritually bankrupt they really were.

Eventually both of their sons married pagan women, a direct violation of God's law. In fact, Elimelech made the wrong decision when he left Judah. He should have confessed his sins and the sins of Israel and then stayed and trusted God to take care of them.

An even greater tragedy lay ahead. Elimelech died and left Naomi as a widow in a land of idolaters. Then both sons died, adding to her desolation.

Knowing what we do about Naomi from the book of Ruth as well as from the larger story of Israel, we can conjecture that she probably didn't want to leave Bethlehem in the first place; but in her cultural situation, she would have had little to say about the decision. As a dutiful wife, she recognized Elimelech as her patriarchal leader. She was duty bound to follow him. The fact was, she had no choice.

Here she was in a land of strangers. She had no ties to her Jewish roots. She was brokenhearted and even bitter. She knew that as a family they had deserted the God of their fathers, and now she felt deserted by God. Her attitudes and feelings are understandable.

Returning to the Heart of God

Naomi eventually came to grips with her plight and faced the reality of what had happened. She decided to return to Bethlehem, to her relatives and her friends and to her sacred opportunity to worship the God of Abraham, Isaac and Jacob in the holy sanctuary.

Initially, she determined to go back alone, to leave behind her daughters-in-law, Ruth and Orpah. In her mind, she was probably attempting to cut all ties with paganism. But both widows wanted to go with Naomi, although Orpah finally decided to stay and continue in her pagan ways. Ruth was different. In the midst of pain and sorrow, she made one of the most beautiful statements of conversion and commitment in all of Scripture. Pleading with Naomi to allow her to return with her to Bethlehem, she promised,

> Where you go I will go, and where you stay I will stay. Your people will be my people *and your God my God* (Ruth 1:16).

Ruth *did* return to Bethlehem and eventually married Boaz, a godly man and a wealthy relative of Naomi. It's a beautiful love story—an experience Ruth had probably not even had with her previous husband, who may have been just as sinful as his father. As Herbert Lockyer states, "There is nothing in the entire range of biography sacred or profane, comparable to the idyllic simplicity, tenderness and beauty of the story of Ruth, the young widow of Moab."[1]

God blessed this new union with a son named Obed, who became the father of Jesse, who in turn became the father of King David. Though a Gentile by birth, Ruth became part of God's chosen line through whom the Savior of the world would be born (see Matt. 1:5-6).

A Woman's Reflections

It's a privilege to introduce you to Ellen Ellwood, who serves along with her husband, Vince, an elder at Fellowship Bible Church North.

Dear Reader,

Fortunately, few of us go through the trials that Naomi endured. But I'm confident that all of us have experienced the ups and downs of a relationship, even with the one we have pledged to love and cherish until death parts us. I know I have.

As I've reflected on Naomi's story, I've been reminded of one of the most helpful biblical truths I've learned personally: All of my needs and expectations cannot be met in one man, my husband; they can only be met in Jesus Christ.

It's Christ who not only loves me but who also wants to love my husband through me. He has been faithful to provide all of the resources I need to love my husband in the good times and in the difficult times. As my husband and I enjoy the good times and together push through the tough ones, it's in turning to God that I continually find guidance and direction. He provides me with strength and insight. He fills the gaps that I have when I am unable to do it on my own. He guides me to solutions. Not surprising, most of the time God's solutions start with changing me.

As you consider the challenges of loving your mate consistently and completely, remember that Christ loves you and lives

in you. He is your advocate. He wants to help you and make
your marriage work to His glory. He understands the needs you
have. He created you to love your husband as only you can! If
you ask Him and trust Him, He will give you the strength and
wisdom to do it!

In Christ's love,
Ellen Ellwood

Learning to Love

Why does Ruth's story set the stage for this quality of maturity outlined by Titus for younger women, to love their husbands? We'd like to answer this question with another. Why did Ruth make such a powerful statement to Naomi when she was about to be left behind? More specifically, why did Ruth say, "Your people will be my people and your God my God"? (Ruth 1:16).

Could it be that Ruth had come to this decision, not only because of her feelings of desolation, but also because of Naomi's faith in the God of her fathers? True, Naomi had followed her husband into a pagan country, and she had watched her sons develop relationships with pagan women—and eventually marry them! But this does not mean that Naomi approved of these decisions. More important, Ruth had watched Naomi love Elimelech regardless of what happened. For the first time in her pagan experience, Ruth may have observed what true love is and, as a result, knew in her heart that Naomi's God was the true God—the gods of wood and stone that she had been taught to worship were not.

The rest of the story affirms that Naomi taught Ruth some valuable lessons about love. She sensibly and wisely advised Ruth in the steps that culminated in her marriage to Boaz. She was indeed an older woman training a younger woman to love her husband. Naomi had grown in her own relationship with God and once again was back in the will of God. As a true daughter of Abraham, she was able to guide Ruth, a young, idol-worshiping Gentile woman, into a personal salvation relationship with her heavenly Father and consequently into a new love relationship—with Boaz. And for the first time in her life, Ruth saw the relationship between a love for God and her love for the special man in her life.

The Cretan Culture

To understand the issues Paul and Titus were facing and addressing, we need to remind ourselves of the pagan culture that permeated the island of Crete. It was not unlike Ruth's environment in Moab. In his letter to Titus, Paul quoted one of the Cretan philosophers, who said, "Cretans are always liars, evil brutes, lazy gluttons" (1:12).

In view of this kind of sinful environment, imagine how men treated women. Though there were some God-fearing Jews living in Crete (see Acts 2:5-11), paganism dominated the culture. Generally speaking, women had no rights and were often treated like slaves.

When the gospel penetrated this culture, whole families often were converted to Christ. However, in some instances, only wives became believers. Perhaps some of the older women Titus was to instruct were Jewish women like Timothy's mother, Eunice, who was committed to God's laws before she became a believer. Eunice lived in Lystra, a very idolatrous city; and in spite of her marriage to a Greek, she had faithfully taught Timothy the Old Testament Scriptures, which laid the foundation for his personal salvation (see Acts 16:1; 2 Tim. 1:5; 3:14-15). Women like Eunice would be wonderful candidates to train younger women to love their husbands.

Then there would be other Jewish women like Naomi, who before becoming believers lived more like their pagan counterparts. However, they at least had a background in Judaism. Once they understood the biblical story of redemption and responded to the gospel, they would be able to model Christlike attitudes and behaviors to young women and to communicate God's true plan for marriage.

This would be particularly important for women whose husbands had not yet responded to the message of salvation. Peter addressed this difficult situation when he wrote, "Wives, in the same way be submissive to your husbands so that, if any of them do not believe the word, they may be won over without words by the behavior of their wives, when they see the purity and reverence of your lives" (1 Pet. 3:1-2).

Understanding Love

One of the first challenges Christian leaders faced in the first-century culture was to help new believers understand God's perspective on love. Having come from a society whose perspective on love was vastly different from God's, the new believers didn't have a clue. Many people in today's society don't have a clue either.

There are at least three important words in the Greek language that we, like they, need to understand in order to have a biblical perspective on love. Though often overlapping in function, each concept is unique.

Agapao Love

The words *agapao* and *agape* are used most frequently in the New Testament to describe love. In most instances these Greek words are used to portray loving *acts*—that is, behaving in certain ways because it is the right thing to do. Jesus Christ demonstrated this kind of love in the ultimate sense when He, with an act of His will, chose the cross. In His humanity, He agonized over this decision. He actually prayed that He might be released from the suffering that lay ahead (see Luke 22:42). However, He knew what His Father's will was, so He died on the cross, though every ounce of human emotion within His being cried out for deliverance. He willingly gave up His life for others. Reflecting on this incredible sacrifice years later, the apostle John wrote, "This is how we know what love is" (1 John 3:16).

To love as Christ loved us is only possible with God's help.

What makes this kind of love so challenging is that we are instructed to "live a life of love, just as Christ loved us and gave himself up for us as a fragrant offering and sacrifice to God" (Eph. 5:2). Obviously, this kind of love is only possible with God's help.

Paul defined agapao love beautifully in 1 Corinthians 13:4-7. Note that all of these reflections of agapao love are actions, not feelings.

> Love is patient, love is kind. It does not envy, it does not boast, it is not proud. It is not rude, it is not self-seeking, it is not easily angered, it keeps no records of wrongs. Love does not delight in evil but rejoices with the truth. It always protects, always trusts, always hopes, always perseveres.

Men and women who converted from the pagan culture of the New Testament world had no concept of this kind of love. Even Jews who had been instructed in the Old Testament Scriptures did not comprehend the love that Jesus Christ would demonstrate when He died on the cross. The gospel of Jesus Christ brought a whole new concept of love: agapao love.

Interestingly, "agapao" was not used often in the Greek and Roman culture. Consequently, it became a very useful and appropriate word for New Testament writers to use in describing Christ's love. Because of the word's infrequent use, they could use it without having to undo a lot of inappropriate associations.

Before older women could train younger women to love their husbands, they had to learn the meaning of this kind of love. Again, the beginning point was to learn from example. Note Paul's reminder when he wrote to the Thessalonians, reflecting on the ministry he and his missionary team had among these people. The majority of them had been converted from a pagan culture; they were people who had "turned to God from idols to serve the living and true God" (1 Thess. 1:9). They had no comprehension regarding agapao love. Paul reminded them, "We loved you so much that we were delighted to share with you not only the gospel of God but our lives as well, because you had become so dear [beloved] to us" (2:8).[2] The Thessalonians never forgot this model. They now knew how to practice this kind of love in their marriage relationships as well as with their children.

Phileo Love

The Greek word *phileo* is often used interchangeably in the New Testament with "agapao," but it is also used distinctively to refer to love that is based on feelings of affection and friendship. Paul described this dimension of love when he wrote to the Romans, "Be devoted to one another in brotherly love" (12:10). The Greek word translated "brotherly love" is *philadelphia,* and it involves the concept of phileo. Paul was using the kind of loving relationships that should exist among family members to illustrate the kind of relationships that should also exist among members of God's family.

In Jesus Christ, husbands and wives are also brothers and sisters. We too are to be devoted to one another in brotherly love. The *King James Version* of the Bible reads, "Be *kindly affectioned* one to another with brotherly love," and the *Holman Christian Standard Bible* reads, "Show family affection to one another with brotherly love."

It's God's will that agapao love and phileo love often blend together. But it's also His will that when warm feelings are absent, we still respond to each other with actions that are Christlike.

Erao Love

The verb for love that was used very frequently by Greek-speaking people in the first century was the word *erao* or "to love sexually." However, New Testament authors never used this word. This does not mean that sexual love is in itself sinful or improper or is never referred to in Scripture. In fact, Paul made it very clear to the Corinthians that to withhold this kind of love from a marital partner is in itself a violation of God's will (see 1 Cor. 7:1-6). However, biblical authors avoided using this word, perhaps because it was so frequently used in the Greek and Roman culture to refer to what God describes as illicit sexual activity. Erotic experience, nevertheless, is a God-created gift that He designed for marriage. Without it, this relationship will never be what God intended it to be. It's that dimension of our personalities that enables a man and woman to be emotionally attracted to each other in ways that go beyond feelings of friendship.

Unfortunately, like the first-century culture, our present culture in many respects defines love in emotional and sexual terms. The words of most popular songs that speak of male-female relationships are clearly focused on sexual feelings. Most movies, books and magazines that feature relationships between men and women also focus on this kind of love. Consequently, when a man says to a woman, "I love you," and the woman says, "I love you too," the essence of their feelings at that moment is frequently sexual. And more recently in our own culture, this kind of definition of love is openly featured in homosexual relationships.

In summary, the Scriptures define love as three-dimensional. *Agapao* love is doing what is right and best for someone, even if it involves negative feelings (see figure 2). *Phileo* love is responding to someone's needs affectionately and with positive emotions, but always within the moral guidelines of agapao love. *Erao* love is becoming both emotionally and physically involved with another person sexually, but always within the guidelines of agapao and phileo love. Regardless of the cultural definitions and societal standards, it's God's will that this kind of love be limited to marriage between a man and a woman.

FIGURE 2

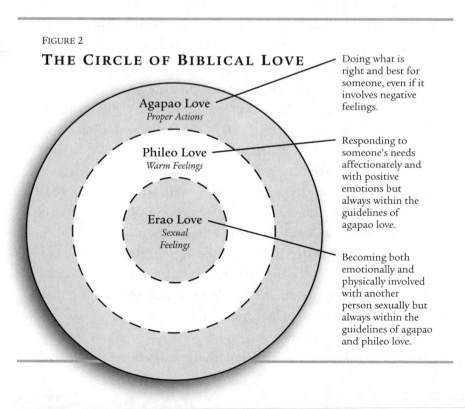

THE CIRCLE OF BIBLICAL LOVE — Doing what is right and best for someone, even if it involves negative feelings.

Agapao Love
Proper Actions

Phileo Love
Warm Feelings — Responding to someone's needs affectionately and with positive emotions but always within the guidelines of agapao love.

Erao Love
Sexual Feelings — Becoming both emotionally and physically involved with another person sexually but always within the guidelines of agapao and phileo love.

A Closer Look

In view of this total biblical perspective, let's look more closely at what Paul was saying to Titus about teaching older women so that they could train younger women to love their husbands.

The word "train" that Paul used in Titus 2:4 definitely implies a process.[3] And the Greek word for love that Paul used here, *phil-andros,* refers to phileo love. As we've seen, this term often refers to the emotional dimensions of love: to friendship and affection in a relationship.

Clearly Paul was teaching that a wife can learn to feel warm and secure in her husband's presence, that she can develop a deep sense of trust and emotional commitment. This would definitely be a new experience for many first-century wives, since most marriages had never included this dimension before. In fact, in the vignette we shared at the beginning of this chapter, Ruth probably experienced this kind of love for the first time in her new relationship with Boaz.

Two Dynamic Lessons

There are at least two important lessons that emerge from a study of biblical love.

1. Actions take precedence over feelings.
This is a difficult concept to implement in our behavior. For wives, it's not easy to do things they'd rather not do. But life is made up of these demands. They must get up when they'd rather sleep. They must cook meals when they'd rather be watching television. They must wash clothes when they'd rather go shopping.

Men, of course, have the same challenges. They'd rather read the paper than play in the backyard with their children—especially after a hard day at work. They'd rather kick off their shoes and relax in the recliner than mow the lawn.

In many instances, of course, positive feelings follow actions. This is normal. In fact, in many instances positive feelings emerge in the process of doing what we know we must do. This is a part of being human. And to act rightly when we don't feel like it is a reflection of our maturity level.

2. Feelings of affection can be learned.

Many women in the New Testament who had converted to Christ had to learn for the first time what it meant to enjoy a relationship with their husbands. Affection *can* be learned. Paul certainly implied this in his instructions to Titus. In most instances, affection is learned through both *example* and *experience*. When people we admire demonstrate affection in their behavior, it is in itself a motivational factor to do the same. And the very experience of sharing affection in the context of acceptance and security also helps to develop this positive emotion.

A Twenty-First-Century Case Study

Lucy has been married for 15 years. She's a Christian and so is her husband, Dave. Lucy has tried to be a good Christian wife and still wants to be; but over the years she has, to use her own words, "fallen out of love" with Dave. Yes, she still respects him and submits to his authority (at least outwardly), but inwardly she doesn't feel attracted to him. In fact, she often finds herself resenting him. Though she hates to admit it, she's most happy when he's not around.

In their intimate life, Lucy has been dutiful because the Bible says she should be. Most of the time she endures the relationship, though at times she admits to some physical satisfaction. Emotionally, however, she feels no real oneness with Dave. She could live without the physical relationship because the emotional satisfaction disappeared a long time ago. In fact, the emotional resentments are so often overpowering that she rarely enjoys the physical relationship.

In reflecting on this case study, we must remind ourselves that there are some problems in the twenty-first century that Scripture does not seem to deal with specifically. True, the Bible tells us what we *should* do and in some instances gives us some clues about *how* to do it, but in other instances we must be creative within basic guidelines.

For example, it is one thing for women to develop feelings of love when they've never had these feelings before—women such as those in the New Testament world. But it's a different problem if a wife has had affectionate feelings toward her husband and then has lost those feelings. To relearn this kind of love is far more difficult than to learn it the first time. It definitely takes more commitment and effort. In essence, the Bible teaches that all of us (both husbands and wives) can learn to love our mates in all three dimensions. This is possible because of Christ's love for us and because of the presence of the Holy Spirit in our lives. Paul made this truth clear in his letter to the Romans: "God has poured out his love into our hearts by the Holy Spirit, whom he has given us" (5:5).

Thinking and Growing Together

The following questions are designed for group discussion after reading and studying the content of this chapter:

- Based on this study, how can Lucy develop positive feelings for her husband once again?

- How can older women train younger women to love their husbands in our culture today?
- What advice would you give to husbands for helping their wives to respond to them emotionally and how can wives communicate these suggestions to their husbands without their husbands' feeling threatened?
- How does Paul's prayer and doxology in Ephesians 3:14-21 relate to this discussion?
- About what can the group pray for you personally?

Set a Goal

Write out one goal you would like to achieve as a result of this study.

Loving Your Children

To love their . . . children
TITUS 2:4

A Biblical Portrait of Eunice, a Dedicated Mother

There is no better example in Scripture to illustrate this quality than Timothy's mother, Eunice. Though Jewish she had married a Gentile (see Acts 16:1). And even though much of the population

where she lived, in Lystra, worshiped Greek gods, she never com-
promised her beliefs. She was a woman of faith, even before she
became a believer. Interestingly, she had seen this faith demonstrated in the life of her own mother, Lois (see 2 Tim. 1:5). Following
Lois's example, when Eunice's son Timothy was old enough to
understand, she began teaching him the holy Scriptures.

From Faith to Faith

Eunice apparently became a believer when Paul and Barnabas came
to Lystra on their first missionary journey. It was there that Paul
healed a crippled man who had been lame from birth. The crowds
were so impressed that they concluded that two Greek gods, Zeus
and Hermes, became incarnated through Paul and Barnabas. In
fact, they began to worship these two missionaries, the exact opposite reaction Paul and Barnabas had anticipated. Ironically, a group
of unbelieving Jews followed them from Antioch and Iconium and
turned the crowds against them. Focusing their hostility on Paul,
they grabbed him, dragged him outside the city and stoned him.
Thinking he was dead, his persecutors returned to the city, but
Luke recorded that a group of disciples—believers in Jesus Christ—
gathered around him. To their amazement, Paul "got up and went
back into the city" (Acts 14:20).

At that moment, Eunice no doubt was among these believers,
perhaps having already put her faith in Jesus as the Messiah. We can
also imagine that her son, Timothy, was standing with her in that
circle of disciples. Whatever the case, when Paul returned to Lystra
on his second missionary journey, Timothy was already a young
believer who had already developed a strong reputation among the
leaders of the Church, both in Lystra and Iconium (see Acts 16:1-2).

A Mother's Great Reward

While visiting with the believers at Lystra and Iconium, Paul
decided that Timothy would make a great missionary compan-

ion (see Acts 16:3). Eunice evidently agreed, as did her unsaved husband. Otherwise Paul would certainly have not allowed Timothy to violate his father's wishes in favor of Timothy's own.

Timothy became Paul's constant and faithful companion for a number of years. And when Paul faced martyrdom in a Roman dungeon, he penned his final letter to Timothy, his son in the faith. It's in this letter that we catch a wonderful glimpse of the mother who dearly loved her son. And because Eunice did, she had prepared Timothy's young heart to receive the gospel message. Listen to Paul's words to Timothy—which are in reality a tribute to Timothy's mother:

> But as for you, continue in what you have learned and have become convinced of, because you know those from whom you learned it, and how from infancy you have known the holy Scriptures, which are able to make you wise for salvation through faith in Christ Jesus (2 Tim. 3:14-15).

A Woman's Reflections

It's a privilege to introduce you to Clarice Harris, who served along with her late husband, Jim, who ministered for many years as an elder at Fellowship Bible Church North.

Dear Reader,

As I read the biblical portrait of Eunice, I was reminded of my own upbringing. My mom and dad were good people, but I never heard them tell me they loved me. In fact, I never heard them say those words to each other.

Fortunately, I married a man who grew up in a very loving family. Not only did they say, "I love you" to one another, but they also expressed it with wonderful, warm hugs.

Frankly, I learned to really love my children and to express that love because I learned it from my husband. I remember how easy it became to teach them about Jesus and His love for them. As I rocked them, holding them in my arms, I sang the wonderful song "Jesus Loves Me."

Let me encourage you as you read this chapter to think carefully about the practical principles for becoming a loving mother to your children. They are biblical as well as practical. And like me, you may need reparenting. If your husband does not know how to express love, you may need older women to train you how to love your children. Seek out women who will encourage you, pray for you and reach out a helping hand when you are struggling. Don't allow Satan to defeat you because at times you find it difficult to be the mother you really want to be!

In Christ's love,
Clarice Harris

The First-Century Setting

The cultural situation in the New Testament world was far different from what it is in our twenty-first-century Western world. So were the emotional dynamics. Just as young wives had difficulty loving their husbands, so also young mothers had difficulty loving their children. Thus Paul had to write to Titus, encouraging him to teach the older women to train the younger women to love not only their husbands but their children as well (see Titus 2:3-4).

The phrase in our English translation "to love their . . . children" actually comes from one Greek word, *philoteknos*, which literally means to be child lovers. As in the previous instruction to learn to love their husbands, Paul again used phileo love, which definitely includes the emotional dimensions in human relationships. Many of the women who came to Christ in New Testament days had to learn to love their children.

These young women probably had difficulty loving their children for the same reasons they had difficulty loving their husbands. Though bearing children was a status symbol for women in the Roman world, a child born as a result of dutiful performance didn't set a very good stage for a love relationship between mother and child. And as is true today, a wife's resentment toward her husband could have easily extended to her children.

We must also remember that women in the first century were little different in their emotional makeup from women in the twenty-first century. Cultural factors certainly alter our emotional nature, yet as human beings we are constructed pretty much the same all over the world and at any moment in history. In other words, the resentments women may have had toward their children may have come about for varying reasons, but the emotional reactions were probably pretty much the same as those that the average woman today experiences. What women feel now is pretty much what women felt then.

Principles for Growth

How can a woman learn to love her children? The following are some principles to help her develop this capacity.

1. Negative feelings under certain circumstances are normal, even for mature Christian women.

The pressures of family life, particularly when children are young, are very real. Life with small children in the home is 24/7. At no other time and in no other situation will there be as much physical and emotional drain on a mother. And for a new mother, these pressures are complicated and intensified by the fact that her role is new to her. She takes her responsibilities very seriously, and as a Christian, her natural sense of responsibility becomes even more acute through her knowledge of biblical expectations. There is no more threatening thought to a young woman—particularly in the Christian community—than the prospect of being a failure as a mother. Most face this mental obsession sometime during the early years of motherhood.

We must also realize that physical strain has a tendency to make a mother vulnerable to emotional difficulties. Furthermore, emotional stress invariably leads to feelings of resentment. And particularly for a Christian, hostile emotions lead to guilt and depression, which in turn create a vicious cycle leading to more guilt and recurring depression.

Every young woman needs to understand these pressures and the natural tendencies toward resentment. To have periodic negative emotions, such as resentment towards young children in the home, is normal. Generally these emotions do not indicate a lack of real love for the child any more than experiencing periodic negative emotions toward a husband means a wife doesn't really love him at the agapao level (see figure 2 in chapter 6). To understand these emotions and why they occur helps a person accept the feelings and avoid the nagging guilt that inevitably makes the problem worse.

Both of us remember an event at a Christian family camp where we were ministering. It happened at the evening meal. A father had become ill during the day, leaving his young wife to manage several young and very active children. We could see that she was at her wit's end. She was desperately trying to manage the situation but was losing control. The children were simply being children, and they were also tired and hungry—just like all of us. Of course, knowing she was becoming the center of attention for everyone in the dining room certainly didn't help this young mother feel secure. Suddenly, the dam that held back the tears broke.

Our daughter-in-law, who had children of her own, sensed this woman's predicament and frustration. She quietly slipped away from our table, sat down beside this mother and began to help bring the children under control. Seeing what was happening, several other young mothers also offered help. We'll never forget the relief that came to that mother's heart.

2. Young women need help from older women.

This is why Paul told Titus to teach the older women to train the younger women. And this is why we have emphasized an older woman's example in this process. Lois, Timothy's grandmother, was evidently this kind of example to her daughter, Eunice. All young women need mature adult models. They're looking for it and they want it.

Just recently, I (Elaine) was talking with a woman with whom I used to meet years ago. At that time, the woman had just become a new mother. I, being older, had been a bit farther down the road with my own children. I couldn't specifically remember what I had shared in those spontaneous moments, so I was rather overwhelmed at how

To be a good mentor for younger women, you must not forget what it was like to go through those early years of motherhood.

much of our conversations regarding child rearing and "wifeology" this mother remembered. In fact, the woman introduced me to some other women as her mentor. I was surprised, but I sensed that this woman was sincere.

There's a lesson for older women here as well. Older women must not forget what it was like to go through those early years of motherhood. They must be careful not to develop an idealism that is removed from reality. Rather than easing the burden of anxiety and guilt by letting young women know you experienced the same emotions, you will only accentuate their problem by telling them not to feel that way and by giving them the impression that mature people don't have these problems.

An older woman must remember, first of all, that she can't change a younger woman's feelings by telling her not to feel that way. Second, she won't be helping if she gives the impression that these feelings are abnormal. Third, she would be dishonest if she were to give the impression that she had never had these difficulties when indeed she really did.

If indeed you happen to be an older woman who rarely experienced negative feelings toward your small children, you're probably the exception, not the rule. If these feelings were minimal, there were probably some very significant reasons why this was true: a very understanding husband, unusual help from someone else in carrying out your responsibilites, a completely different environment, etc. If you're going to be a good trainer of and mentor for younger women, you must not forget your own experiences. If your feelings and experiences were different from the norm, then you must understand what those differences were.

3. More than ever, cultural trends can be devastating to family life.

The women's movement in our culture is only one trend that has made devastating inroads into the average American family. Combined with this are the trends of secularism, materialism and sensualism. Everywhere a woman turns she's bombarded with a value system that is eating away at what God ordained to be a very fulfilling and rewarding lifestyle.

Young women in our society are taught to be professionally oriented throughout their academic experiences. Consequently, many women are psychologically prepared to pursue a professional career rather than become a homemaker.

All of us, both men and women, must understand the influence that culture has on our personalities. We cannot ignore it. Together, husband and wife must face the reality of this problem and, within the context of Christian principles, work toward a satisfactory solution.

4. A biblical perspective on motherhood is vital.

The Bible clearly teaches that "children are a gift of the LORD" (Ps. 127:3, *NASB*). In fact, the Scriptures seem to teach that, for women, having children is one of God's major plans for fulfillment. Thus Paul, when discussing the effects of the Fall on women's status in life, wrote something that is rather difficult to understand out of context. He said, "Women will be saved through childbearing—if they continue in faith, love and holiness with propriety" (1 Tim. 2:15).

What Paul meant by this statement has been the subject of a lot of discussion. Obviously, he did not mean a woman finds eternal salvation through producing children. This would be totally contradictory to the whole of Scripture. Rather, it seems he was saying that a woman, even though she has been affected negatively by the Fall, finds her most significant fulfillment by experiencing the rewards of being a wife and mother.

If a woman turns her life totally over to God, she can be "saved" from the competitive problems of a male-dominated culture, in which the male ego is also desperately affected by sin in the world. She will be saved from the loneliness and frustration that often accompany a career. She will be saved from the false ideologies that elevate career and disparage motherhood and that eventually lead to lingering disappointment and disillusionment.

Of course, this doesn't mean that a woman cannot be fulfilled without children or a husband. Furthermore, it doesn't mean that a mother can't continue in a career under certain circumstances. Let's remember too that Paul commended singlehood for those who feel led this way (see 1 Cor. 7:8,32-35). The point is that many in today's world are attempting to communicate that having children—being a wife and mother—can never lead to fulfillment. This is in direct contradiction to the Scriptures and runs counter to God's principles.

Twenty-First-Century Case Studies

Jim and Susan

Jim and Susan had been married for three years. When they first got married, they decided to postpone having children for about five years so that Jim could complete graduate school and become a full-fledged accountant.

Susan worked as an executive secretary. She loved her work and was making good money to help put her husband through school. She also took a few graduate courses at night at the same university Jim attended. In fact, twice a week they met for dinner in the school cafeteria.

But then it happened. She became pregnant two years before their target date. Obviously, they had to change their plans radically. Susan dropped out of school immediately and then quit work during her sixth month of pregnancy. She's now very much occupied at home as a young mother.

Jim curtailed his study schedule drastically to earn enough money to care for his family. This meant postponing his graduation for a couple of years. Immediately Susan sensed Jim's disappointment. She felt he blamed her for the pregnancy. And she had to admit her own disappointment. She resented having to drop out of school and give up her job, and down deep she resented Jim's attitude.

Today Susan has a chronic problem. Little Jim, Jr., is now two, and every day Susan fights feelings of resentment toward her little boy. His daily needs and constant demands on her time are a persistent reminder of her earlier disappointment and negative feelings. To make matters worse, she feels guilty about resenting her son. All of this, of course, affects her relationship with her husband, Jim.

Bob and Mary

Mary's case is quite different. Ever since she can remember, she looked forward to having children. She actually worked in the church nursery as a teenager because she loved babies.

But now, after four years of marriage, she has three children of her own, aged one, two and three. Beginning a family so soon and having one each year was actually her idea. Her husband, Bob, wanting to please her, certainly had no objections. But things are different now. Changing diapers in the church nursery was one thing; but doing it every day, several times a day and for three children—well, that's another story. Her three little, needy children are beginning to drive her up the wall.

Bob isn't as understanding as he used to be either. When he gets home from work, Mary is exhausted, the home is in shambles, and dinner isn't even started. To meet Bob's emotional and physical needs has become a real problem for Mary. By the end of the evening, she is so tired that she falls asleep the moment her head hits the pillow, leaving Bob feeling neglected and rejected.

Actually, Mary is beginning to resent Bob, blaming him for her predicament, even though it was her idea originally to have three children a year apart. Also, she's experiencing constant negative emotions toward the children. She finds herself resenting them deeply and blaming them for interfering with her ability to be a good wife to Bob. Furthermore, she feels she never has any time to herself, which is all too obvious. Her idealism has turned into a demanding routine that is leaving her feeling frustrated, angry and, of course, guilty—which eventually ends up in depression.

Tom and Nancy

Nancy's case is different still. She has been married 20 years and has 4 children—all girls, aged 9, 12, 15 and 17. Generally, she was a happy person, a good mother and a diligent homemaker—until three years ago when she made a couple of new friends.

Nancy's new friends invited her to a special meeting to hear a woman speak on women's rights, and things she never really thought about before began to surface in her mind and emotions. Since that meeting, she has read articles and books and has listened to more speakers; now she is convinced that she is an unfulfilled woman. The reason, of course, revolves around her "wasted years."

Nancy now resents the time spent with her children. In fact, she resents her children themselves. They are still dependent on her, which frustrates her. *Obviously, they are interfering with my desire to go back to school in order to prepare myself for a good job and a fulfilling position,* Nancy thinks to herself. Nancy is determined that she is going to make up for lost time, no matter what happens to her family.

Nancy's husband, Tom, is bewildered. He doesn't know what to do. Down deep he's afraid that Nancy is going to ask for a divorce.

These stories are based on real situations in today's world. More than at any other moment in our history, Satan is attempting to destroy the family. The number of marriages ending in divorce is staggering. Unfortunately, children are often the ones most hurt by divorce. By God's grace, we must do all we can to reverse this trend! With God's strength and help from other mature Christians, we can defeat Satan—beginning now!

If you are a single woman, perhaps these case studies will help prepare you for marriage and motherhood. You indeed can become a model in this area of Christian living.

Thinking and Growing Together

The following suggestions are designed for group discussion after reading and studying the content of this chapter:

- What should Jim and Susan do to head off a potential tragedy in their marriage and family life?
- If you were counseling Bob and Mary, what advice would you give them?
- In Nancy's situation, how might her decisions affect her marriage and those of her daughters in the future?
- How can the average young mother in our culture find relief from the responsibilities and pressure of child rearing?
- About what can the group pray for you personally?

Set a Goal

Write out one goal you would like to achieve as a result of this study.

Being Wise and Sensible

To be self-controlled

A Biblical Portrait of Abigail and Nabal, the Beauty and the Beast

There are some men who are married to women they don't deserve! Nabal, an extremely wealthy farmer, was one of these men. His wife's name was Abigail and the Scriptures mince no words in contrasting her personality and character with her husband's: "She was an intelligent and beautiful woman, but her husband, a Calebite, was surly and mean in his dealings" (1 Sam. 25:3).

Abigail's story appears in the Old Testament because of David. Before David became the king of Israel and while he was still being pursued by Saul, he and his 600 men set up headquarters in the same area where Abigail's husband, Nabal, grazed his sheep. David demonstrated unusual kindness to Nabal's shepherds—never harassing them and always protecting them from other intruders (see vv. 15-16).

A Personal Agenda

It is apparent that David also had an agenda: to feed 600 men. And being a shepherd himself, he knew that sheepshearing time would be the moment to ask for assistance. Culturally, this festive occasion was a time to show hospitality. Consequently, he sent two men to ask for help. They were to greet Nabal graciously in David's name and remind him of the way they had protected his shepherds.

Nabal's response was brash and the ultimate snub. He hurled the greatest insult at David any man could ever give another. Knowing full well the amazing story about Goliath, as well as Saul's jealous episodes, he responded with arrogance: "Who is this David? Who is this son of Jesse? Many servants are breaking away from their masters these days" (v. 10).

Anger Out of Control

Predictably, David was infuriated. He grabbed his sword and ordered 400 men to do the same. Right then and there he vowed he would kill every man associated with Nabal—which no doubt included Nabal himself (see vv. 13,21-22).

One of Nabal's servants predicted what was going to happen when he observed the way Nabal treated David's men.

Knowing that Abigail would quickly grasp what was about to transpire, he lost no time in telling her the whole story (see vv. 14-17). Fortunately, she was Nabal's opposite—wise, sensible and discerning.

A Peace Offering

Abigail quickly prepared enough food to feed an army and went out to meet David. As she approached him, she humbly fell at his feet, taking the blame for Nabal's irresponsible actions. Begging for mercy, she reminded David that to follow through on his plan to kill her husband and his servants would be an overwhelming burden on David's conscience (see vv. 18,23-31).

Abigail's wisdom paid off. Just as quickly as David had lost control of his emotions, he regained perspective. He was humbled by this woman's openness and honesty. More important, he saw God's hand at work. Responding with gratitude, he blessed God and Abigail:

> Praise be to the LORD, the God of Israel, who has sent you today to meet me. May you be blessed for your *good judgment* and for keeping me from bloodshed this day and from avenging myself with my own hands (vv. 32-33).

Herbert Lockyer captured what happened that day. Commenting on Abigail's wisdom, he said: "Possessing heavenly intelligence, self-control, common sense and vision, she exercised boundless influence over a great man, and marked herself out as a truly great woman."[1]

Nabal's Sad Demise

When Abigail returned home, she found her husband so drunk that he couldn't carry on an intelligent conversation. But in the morning when he was sober, Abigail was just as honest with

Nabal as she had been with David. She told him exactly what had happened. The text of Scripture is very graphic: traumatized with either anger or fear, or both, "[Nabal's] heart failed him and he became like a stone" (v. 37). Nabal never recovered. In 10 days, he was dead (see vv. 36-38).

An Ironic Ending

If the final scene in this dramatic story were staged in a Verdian opera, it might be called "A Twist of Fate." When David heard about Nabal's death, he sent a proposal to Abigail and asked her to become his wife. Apparently, it didn't take much thought on her part to respond. What makes this so ironic is that Nabal not only lost his life but also his wife, who then married the man he refused to help (see vv. 39-42)!

Some have named this story "The Beauty and the Beast." Abigail *was* a beautiful woman, both inside and out. Though her husband often acted like a selfish fool and in his drunken stupors probably treated her badly, there is no indication that she ever contemplated leaving him. She simply tried to keep peace in the household and often had to clean up the messes he created.

A Woman's Reflections

It's a privilege to introduce you to Charlotte Lindgren, who serves along with her husband, Earl, an elder at Fellowship Bible Church North.

Dear Reader,

When I think of a woman who is wise and sensible and exercises self-control, I'm reminded of my good friend Jeanie. In her late 20s, she married a man who already had two very young daughters. Then, a few years later, Jeanie and her husband had two boys of their own. There were sibling issues as well as stress on their marriage as a result of the blended families. There were repeated circumstances when she had to control her own responses in heated situations and use discretion and wisdom. Over the years, I repeatedly witnessed Jeanie's godly response and the love she exhibited in each trying circumstance. She firmly believed in the truth of Ephesians 1:11 (NLT): "[God] chose us from the beginning, and all things happen just as he decided long ago."

It was evident that she was secure in her relationship with her Savior and drew strength from that bond, which enabled her to accept each trial as from God and working for her good (see Rom. 8:28). The best part was watching her mature spiritually over the years, and I believe it was largely a result of all the tests God allowed in her life. At the time, she didn't always understand, but she always wanted to see God's hand on her life and the lives of her husband and children. Yes, she had some dark days, but she never let them overshadow her future. Her roots reached "deep into the water" as we read in Jeremiah 17:8 (NLT). That reality gave her the wisdom and self-control to face those difficult situations with grace and good sense.

I encourage any woman to tap God's resources when confronted with difficult circumstances. It is so important to hide God's Word in your heart (see Ps. 119:11) before you meet the obstacles. Then, the Holy Spirit can bring those verses immediately back to your remembrance at the right time. It's much more difficult, and there's often not enough time, to begin searching for the right Scripture when you're in the midst of a trial. I urge you to set aside a part of each day to memorize Scripture—even if it's only one verse. You'll be glad you did when the next test comes along.

Prayerfully yours,
Charlotte Lindgren

Wise and Sensible

We chose Abigail's story since Abigail modeled self-control in a very difficult situation. The Greek term *sophron* literally means "sound in mind."[2] Various Bible versions also translate the word as "discreet," "sober," "wise" and "sensible," depending on the context in which it is used.

Paul exhorted all believers to be self-controlled more than any other characteristic of maturity. Notice that in his letter to Titus, he referred to this characteristic three times to indicate his concern that both men and women of all ages develop this quality of maturity in their lives:

- "Teach the older men to be temperate, worthy of respect, *self-controlled*" (2:2).
- "Likewise, teach the older women . . . to teach what is good. Then they can train the younger women to love their husbands and children, to be *self-controlled*" (2:3-5).
- "Similarly, encourage the young men to be *self-controlled*" (2:6).

When Paul stated that he wanted older women to train younger women to be self-controlled, what did he have in mind? There are at least three characteristics mentioned in Scripture that reflect this basic quality.

1. A self-controlled woman is a humble woman.

One of our favorite passages of Scripture, which illustrates and explains what Paul had in mind when he used the word "self-control" to describe maturity, is what he wrote to the Romans:

For by the grace given me I say to every one of you: Do not think of yourself more highly than you ought, but rather think of yourself with *sober judgment* [*sophroneo*], in accordance with the measure of faith God has given you (12:3).

Here, of course, Paul was addressing the whole Body of Christ. We are to be self-controlled in terms of how we view ourselves in relationship to God and to other Christians (see vv. 4-8). We are not to have an exalted view of our position in the Body of Christ. This is why Paul went on to say:

Be devoted to one another in brotherly love. Honor one another above *yourselves* (v. 10).

Similarly, Paul wanted younger women to realize that all of their gifts, abilities and possessions came from God. Without Him, they could not speak or walk or make decisions or even breathe. He wanted them to practice what he wrote to the Philippian Christians:

Do nothing out of selfish ambition or vain conceit, but in *humility* consider others better than yourselves. Each of you should look not only to your own interests, but also to the interests of others (Phil. 2:3-4).

Abigail, even in an Old Testament setting, demonstrated this kind of character. Deeply concerned about her household—and even about her insensitive husband—she humbled herself before David, falling at his feet and actually taking the blame for Nabal's arrogant and selfish behavior (see 1 Sam. 25:23-24). Nabal's actions, of course, were just the opposite of being self-controlled. Nabal was proud, arrogant and stupid.

2. A self-controlled woman is motivated by God's grace.
Paul set the example of a person motivated by God's grace,

God's unmerited favor, which brings salvation to all of us. Paul never forgot how God reached out to him with the salvation message when he was on his way to Damascus to persecute Christians. He wanted younger women to be taught and disciplined by grace, which included living self-controlled lives. Applying this truth to all believers a few paragraphs later in Titus, Paul wrote:

> For the grace of God that brings salvation has appeared to all men [and women]. It teaches us to say "No" to ungodliness and worldly passions, and to live *self-controlled*, upright and godly lives in this present age (2:11-12).

3. A self-controlled woman understands the relationship between self-control and prayer.
The apostle Peter taught this correlation when he wrote:

> The end of all things is near. Therefore be clear minded and *self-controlled* so that you can *pray* (1 Peter 4:7).

Arrogant and foolish people are so wrapped up in themselves that they normally never ask for help. They have such an exalted view of their human capabilities and their sense of power over others that they act impulsively, just like Nabal did. Fortunately, Nabal's wife was clear minded enough to know that she needed help from the one person who could save her household—David. By asking, she received!

Today, as Christians, we can become so self-absorbed and self-sufficient that we believe we can solve all of our problems by ourselves. Paul wanted these young women in Crete to be clear minded and self-controlled, enabling them to look beyond themselves for help in knowing how to relate to their husbands and their children. Ultimately, God was the One who could offer them the help they needed. But as He often does, He carries on His purposes through other Christians in our lives—in this case, godly older women.

Twenty-First-Century Case Studies

Jane
From the first day Jane arrived on the scene, everyone got the distinct impression that she felt she was God's gift to the church. Everyone she talked to heard about her participation and achievements in other Christian circles: She sang solos, played the piano and taught a variety of Sunday School classes, and the clincher, she knew Billy Graham personally. (The truth is that she had maneuvered herself into a receiving line on one occasion when he was greeting people and shook his hand.) In fact, Jane name-dropped all the time.

Jane's problem has at least two possible explanations. On the one hand, she may have been in the limelight all her life. This experience created a psychological need to perform and be recognized. On the other hand, she may have been deprived of love and attention as a youngster. This led her to put herself down. Now she feels she has to compensate by striving for personal achievement that competes with others. But whatever the source of the problem, the outer manifestation is pride and lack of self-control in this area of her life.

Paul, in his letter to Titus, was saying that a woman like Jane needs a good parental model, preferably an older godly woman who understands Jane's problem and can help her understand herself and become more Christlike in her behavior.

Meredith

Meredith's problem is the opposite of Jane's, at least in its out-ward manifestation. She constantly withdraws from others and feels inferior. When people reach out to her, she feels uncom-fortable. She's afraid she'll say the wrong thing, causing others to dislike her. Unfortunately, some people often misinterpret Meredith's behavior. They conclude that she wants to be alone. Others believe that she feels that she's too good to be around them.

Timothy could probably identify with Meredith's problem. He too was timid and fearful. Consequently, Paul had to encourage him with these words, "For God did not give us a spirit of timid-ity, but a spirit of power, of love and of self-discipline" (2 Tim. 1:7). "Self-discipline" is translated from the Greek word *sophron-ismos*, which also means "self-control."[3]

In reality, Timothy had nothing to be ashamed of. He had a good heritage—a weak father perhaps, but a godly mother and grandmother (see 2 Tim. 1:5; 3:14-15). He was one of God's choice servants and a fellow missionary of the great apostle Paul. There was no reason for Timothy to be timid and fearful. Yet he was! And throughout his life, he needed constant encouragement to live boldly for God. Some feel that his stom-ach problems were psychosomatic in origin, the result of emo-tional difficulties; namely, his fear and timid personality (see 1 Tim. 5:23).

Like Timothy did, Meredith also needs encouragement. Paul implied in his letter to Titus that a godly older woman who is mature in self-control and humility can serve as the best means to help Meredith overcome her inferiority complex. In short, she needs Christlike feminine models.

Barbara and Cynthia

Barbara and Cynthia are sisters. Both are newly married. And both have focused on material things to attract attention to themselves but in different ways.

Barbara dresses extravagantly, often driving her husband to a state of anger. She spends money beyond their means, buying expensive clothes and jewelry that she wears on rare occasions. Her desire to impress other people, particularly other women, seems almost insatiable.

Cynthia's problem, though related to Barbara's in its roots, manifests itself somewhat differently. Like Barbara, Cynthia is obsessed with impressing others, but the objects of her attention-getting behavior are men. She also is extravagant in her spending, but her grooming habits concentrate on being seductive. She knows that she can get the eyes of other men and she consciously schemes to achieve that goal. Not surprisingly, her husband is threatened by this behavior. At the same time, she is very cold and insensitive toward him at home, yet in public she acts seductively toward him to get the attention of other men.

The apostle Paul warned Christian women against this kind of behavior. He used the word *sophrosune* (self-control and personal discipline)[4] when he wrote, "I also want women to dress modestly, with decency and *propriety*, not with braided hair or gold or pearls or expensive clothes, but with good deeds, appropriate for women who profess to worship God" (1 Tim. 2:9-10).

Don't misunderstand! Paul was not saying a woman should not make herself beautiful. What he is warning against is materialistic behavior that is based on self-centered, seductive attitudes. He was speaking to women who were *not* self-controlled in this area of their lives. Their need for attention was so strong that they lost perspective, even in the area of Christian morality and what is indeed "appropriate for women who profess to worship God."

It's possible that both Barbara and Cynthia were neglected as children. When all the other little girls wore pretty dresses and experienced normal acceptance and praise, Barbara and Cynthia stood out as being different. Now they're compensating, one in one way and the other in another. But the results are the same emotionally. They feel that they are getting the attention they lacked as children.

By biblical standards, both actions are wrong, even though they have understandable but explainable psychological roots. Both Barbara and Cynthia need to become self-controlled, to become godly women who are mature in Jesus Christ. And again, they need the example of older Christian women who can train them to develop this quality.

Thinking and Growing Together

The following questions are designed for group discussion after reading and studying the content of this chapter:

- As you reflect on the case studies in this chapter, what other reasons may cause a woman (a) to build herself up like Jane, (b) to withdraw like Meredith or (c) to attract attention to herself like Barbara or Cynthia?
- As you discuss each case study, what advice would you give to each woman to help her solve her problems? What would you suggest to Jane? To Meredith? To Barbara or Cynthia?
- As you review the story of Abigail in 1 Samuel 25, in what ways did this woman demonstrate self-control, even in this Old Testament setting?

· What suggestions do you have to help Christian women
living in the twenty-first century develop self-control?
· About what can the group pray for you personally?

Set a Goal

Write out one goal you would like to achieve as a result of this
discussion.

Living Pure Lives

[To be] pure
TITUS 2:5

A Biblical Portrait of Rahab,
Who Was Purified by Faith

It may seem strange to select a prostitute from Jericho to illustrate Paul's exhortation to Titus to teach the older women in Crete to train the younger women to be pure. When we consider the culture and moral values on this island in the Mediterranean Sea, it's very likely that some of the women who put their faith in Christ in this first-century setting may very well have been engaging in the world's oldest profession, particularly as temple prostitutes. One thing is for sure, all of these women who were converted from paganism had not been trained in their families and in the culture at large to be morally pure as this quality of life is defined in the holy Scriptures.

Consider, for example, the city of Corinth. More than 1,000 women served as priestesses in the Temple of Aphrodite. After the gospel penetrated this licentious city, Paul wrote to the Corinthian believers, outlining a spectrum of immoral activities that characterized these people before they came to faith in Christ.

> Do you not know that the wicked will not inherit the kingdom of God? Do not be deceived: Neither the sexually immoral nor idolaters nor adulterers nor male prostitutes nor homosexual offenders nor thieves nor the greedy nor drunkards nor slanderers nor swindlers will inherit the kingdom of God. *And that is what some of you were. But you were washed, you were sanctified, you were justified in the name of the Lord Jesus Christ and by the Spirit of our God* (1 Cor. 6:9-11).

Rahab's Statement of Faith

Centuries earlier, Joshua sent spies to investigate Jericho, another very pagan and immoral city. The biblical record clearly states that these men "entered the house of a prostitute named Rahab" (Josh. 2:1). Shortly after they had settled in, a surveillance team sent out by the king of Jericho also arrived on the scene. Anticipating this investigation, Rahab had already hidden these men on her roof under stalks of flax.

Rahab's action poses several questions. Why was she so eager to protect these men of Israel? Why was she willing to risk her own life should the spies be discovered? We believe these questions point to one basic answer. Though Rahab is still identified as a prostitute in the biblical text, she had already turned away from idolatry and prostitution and had put her faith in the God of Abraham, Isaac and Jacob.

Note the certainty inherent in Rahab's testimony to the spies after the men from Jericho left her home: "I know that the Lord has given this land to you" (2:9). For 40 years, Rahab had observed the concerns and fears of her own people in Jericho and of the other inhabitants of the land, all of whom were left breathless by the miracles that God had performed for Israel: the parting of the Red Sea and the destruction of the Egyptian army. And more recently, the people of Jericho were awestruck by Israel's great victories over the Amorites on the other side of Jordan (see 2:9-11). They also knew that this God of Israel had revealed that Canaan was the land that He had chosen for these nomadic people who had been wandering in the wilderness for 40 years. And now, Israel was on the march!

But there was a great difference between Rahab and the other Canaanites: She acted on what she knew—she acknowledged that God was the one true God. Her statement of faith was very simple but very specific when she said, "For the LORD your God is God in heaven above and on the earth below" (2:11).

Rahab's Work of Faith

When James wrote his epistle centuries later, he wanted his readers to know that "faith without deeds is dead" (2:26). In other words, faith that does not result in good works reflects no real faith at all. He used Rahab, an Old Testament believer, as an illustration:

> In the same way, was not even *Rahab the prostitute* considered *righteous* for what she did when she gave lodging

to the spies and sent them off in a different direction? (v. 25).

Please understand that James was *not* teaching that either Rahab or we are saved by works. Rather, he was explaining the very same biblical truth that the apostle Paul taught after Paul had emphasized that we are saved by grace through faith—not works—because salvation is God's gift (see Eph. 2:8-9). Paul went on to clarify that "we are God's *workmanship*, created in Christ Jesus to *do good works*, which God prepared in advance for us to do" (v. 10).

The radical changes in Rahab's life illustrate that this woman had truly come to know God through faith, just as Abraham had done years before when he believed God, and God counted it as *righteousness* (see Rom. 4:3). Abraham, an Old Testament man of faith, then went on to demonstrate the reality of that faith when he obeyed God and was willing to sacrifice the life of his son Isaac (see Jas. 2:21).

Reflect for a moment on the additional evidence that Rahab was a true believer and had already changed her profession—maybe years before. How else can we explain the stalks of flax that she had laid in order on the roof of her home (see Josh. 2:6)? Industrious women of noble character would spend hours gathering these stalks to make clothes (see Prov. 31:13). If Rahab had still been practicing her old profession, she wouldn't be out gathering flax. Since she had gathered enough to cover up two grown men, she apparently had been in the cloth business for a significant period of time.

Consider also the scarlet cord (see Josh. 2:17-21). Since it was difficult to store liquid dye for ready use to create various colored fabrics, cloth makers would put lengthy ropes into the various vats of colored dye to absorb the dye. Usually a very small piece of colored rope—six inches or so—would dye a large quantity of cloth. Note that Rahab had accumulated enough rope of only one color to hang over a wall that may have been as high as 30 feet (see v. 15). For a cloth maker in Jericho, that was a great inventory to support a thriving business.

God's Grace

The greatest lesson that emerges from this fascinating event is that God is no respecter of persons. Otherwise, why would He give so much space in the midst of divine history to record Rahab's story? Clearly, God wants all people to know that Jesus Christ died for the sins of the whole world. There's no individual outside the sphere of His love and grace (see John 3:16). This is also why the author of Hebrews still identified Rahab in chapter 11, the New Testament Hall of Faith, as a prostitute (see v. 31). All men and women everywhere, regardless of their moral condition, can call on the name of the Lord and be saved (see Rom. 10:13).

One final question: Why is Rahab included in the genealogy of Jesus (see Matt. 1:5)? This demonstrates in a profound and dynamic way that even though Jesus Christ was the perfect Son of God, in His humanity He can identify with all people—no matter how sordid their lifestyles! He has extended His saving grace to all human beings, including those who are blatantly immoral. But once we become Christians, we're cleansed from all sin (see 1 John 1:9), and it's God's will that from that moment forward we be taught God's moral standard, a standard of purity.

A Woman's Reflections

It's a privilege to introduce you to Maureen Burford, who serves along with her husband, Ed, an elder at Fellowship Bible Church North.

Dear Reader,

Rahab is a wonderful example not only of how God forgives us of our sins but also of how completely He can change and restore our lives and give us back "the years the locusts have eaten" (Joel 2:25). But a story like this should also motivate us to remain pure—particularly as young women.

As my own boldness for the Lord grew, I had the courage to speak frankly with our youngest daughter, Susanna. Beginning in her middle school years, I shared with her the tremendous benefits of staying sexually pure for her future husband. I explained that God's rules are not meant to restrict us but actually to give us the maximum amount of freedom in the long term.

We discussed sexually transmitted diseases, but primarily, I dwelt on how remaining sexually pure would keep her heart from becoming hardened (as a protective measure from many different partners). By remaining chaste, she would have the joy and delight of a beautiful bonding with her husband and the pleasure of a deep friendship with him before that sexual bonding took place. She also would be developing self-control and would be keeping her relationship with God pure.

Since her freshman year in high school, Susanna has chosen to wear a ring promising God to remain sexually pure until her marriage. As she sees friends who have not chosen this commitment, she can tell them how much premarital sex hampers a healthy relationship with their boyfriends. In addition, part of remaining sexually pure also involves a girl's thought life and dressing modestly yet fashionably, so she'll not be unfairly enticing to men.

Perhaps you have daughters or are mentoring teenage girls. Please, let me strongly encourage you to speak openly and honestly about sexual purity and its many benefits and its multitude of pitfalls. If a young girl has slipped, encourage her to confess unreservedly to God and to then begin afresh on the path to remaining *sexually pure. Our lives are the very happiest when we live in harmony with God's principles. If God forgave Rahab, He'll certainly forgive us regardless of our failures. The apostle John wrote, "The blood of Jesus, his Son, purifies us from* all sin,*" and "If we confess our sins, he is faithful and just and will forgive us our sins and purify us* from all unrighteousness*" (1 John 1:7,9).*

Rahab renewed her life with such a pure passion that she is honored by being in the lineage of the Lord Jesus. Though we don't have this privilege, we can by faith become "heirs of God and co-heirs with Christ" (Rom. 8:17).

With joy in the journey,
Maureen Burford

The Hallmark of Maturity

Sexual purity stands out in the pages of the Bible as one of the most important qualities for measuring Christian maturity. The Greek word *hagnos* literally means to be pure from carnality, to be chaste, to be modest.[1]

Paul was concerned that *all* Christian women, young and old alike, maintain pure relationships with men as well as other women. Then and now, women's attitudes and behavior can be more determinative of the standard of purity that will be upheld in relationships than men's. The apostle Peter exhorted Christian men to treat their wives with tenderness and respect because physically they are normally the weaker partners (see 1 Peter 3:7). But when it comes to sexual power and control, women definitely have the upper hand. History is filled with accounts of men who, though rulers over kingdoms and people, were often under the spell of sensual women.

A Biblical Illustration

Consider King Herod of Jesus' day. He was living with his brother Philip's wife, Herodias. No doubt her seductive behavior played a significant part in this very open but illegitimate relationship. John the Baptist spoke out boldly against this immoral arrangement. "It is not lawful for you to have her," he cried out boldly to Herod and for everyone to hear (Matt. 14:4).

Women's sensual actions and sexual favors have brought men from all walks of life to give up fame, fortune and position.

Being a typical man who is involved in immoral behavior, Herod probably rationalized his actions and ignored John's outcry. Not so with Herodias! She became so angry with John that she wanted to kill him.

Herodias's opportunity came one evening when her beautiful daughter was performing a sensuous dance for all the leading men of Galilee: high officials, military commanders and other notables. It was Herod's birthday, and no doubt a combination of alcohol and lust caused him to promise Herodias's daughter anything her heart desired—up to half of his kingdom.

By any standard of measurement, this was a very stupid thing to do. But, this was the moment Herodias was looking for. She moved into action and prompted her daughter to ask for John's head on a platter. Even in his drunken state, Herod knew full well that this was a heinous crime. Yet because of his pride, his weakness and his bondage to a sensual and evil woman,

Herod gave an order for John to be killed (see Matt. 14:1-12; Mark 6:14-29).

How tragic! But how true! Women's sensual actions and sexual favors have brought men from all walks of life to give up fame, fortune and position. In these situations, a woman is definitely *not* the weaker partner.

A Contemporary Illustration

We are reminded of Tony. At one time, he was in Christian work. When he and his lovely wife were getting up in years, he met a girl many years younger than himself, and they became involved sexually. Addicted to the ego satisfaction she gave him, he left his wife, disillusioned his children and openly lied to those who confronted him about his sin. Spiritually, he turned his back on everything he stood for. Psychologically, he was like putty in this young woman's hands. Mentally, his thinking became bazaar and irrational. It was as if he were under a hypnotic spell.

Though God's curse as a result of Eve's sin would cause men to rule over women (see Gen. 3:16)—to control, dominate and abuse them—God did not take away from them the ultimate power over men. Using sex in selfish and sinful ways, every woman has the potential to consistently manipulate a man to her own advantage. Paul warned against this. And by all means, it should never be a part of the lifestyle of a Christian woman. Thus, Paul instructed Titus to teach the older women to train the younger women to be self-controlled and pure.

Unsaved Husbands

What happened in the pagan culture in New Testament times when a woman became a believer and her husband continued on in his pagan ways? The apostle Peter addressed the wives concerning this issue: "Be submissive to your husbands so that, if any of them *do not believe the word,* they may be won over without words by the behavior of their wives, when they see the *purity* and reverence of your lives" (1 Peter 3:1-2).

Lifestyle Witnessing

Knowing Christ as Savior was to bring significant lifestyle changes, particularly in the area of moral values. And though an unbelieving husband in those days may have continued in his sinful ways, Peter instructed wives who became believers to demonstrate marital faithfulness and purity. This, combined with submission and "the unfading beauty of a gentle and quiet spirit" (1 Pet. 3:4), oftentimes became a means whereby an unsaved husband became a Christian.

Though the Scriptures do not guarantee that this approach will always work, in many instances it does—even in the twenty-first century. Inherent in a man is a tendency to respond to a woman who respects him, who is loyal to him and who practices the presence of Jesus Christ.

A Practical Question

What should a Christian woman do if she's married to an unsaved man who continues to be promiscuous and unfaithful after she has become a Christian? How would Peter answer this question today in view of AIDS and many other sexually trans-mitted diseases?

We have faced this problem in our own pastoral ministry. Frankly, we could never in good conscience encourage a wife under these circumstances to continue in a sexual relationship with her husband. She could quite literally be taking her life into her own hands, running the risk of acquiring a sexually transmitted disease. And if she should get pregnant, she could potentially be taking the life of a newborn baby. In cases like this, we've advised the wife to do all she can to respect her husband and to demonstrate her own commitment to moral values. But if a husband does not demonstrate conclusively that he has given up relationships with other women and also refuses to submit to careful testing over a period of time for sexually transmitted diseases, she should then proceed to separate from her husband and, in time, seek a legitimate divorce—if indeed he did not respond and do what is right. We believe this advice is in harmony with the overall teachings of Scripture (see Matt. 5:31-32).

Biblical Guidelines for Sexual Purity

Since we live in a culture in which sexual promiscuity is the norm, we need to know what God teaches about sexual purity. The following are biblical guidelines:

1. A marriage relationship—*Intimate sexual relationships between a man and a woman are to take place within the bonds of a legitimate and recognized marriage.*

This biblical principle runs counter to what are becoming very common views in our own twenty-first-century culture. Think for a moment: How often do you see a Hollywood movie that promotes sexual abstinence until marriage?

Unfortunately, many unmarried, professing Christian couples are engaging in intimate sexual acts, believing that their behavior is acceptable as long as they are involved in a committed relationship. However, the very Bible these couples read and believe to be the Word of God never condones this kind of intimacy outside of a permanent marriage.

Note what the apostle Paul wrote to the Ephesians. Quoting both Moses and Jesus, he explained:

For this reason a man will leave his father and mother and be *united to his wife,* and the two will become one flesh (Eph. 5:31).

Though both the Hebrew and Greek words translated as "wife" can refer to a woman in general, the context definitely signifies a permanent married relationship. A man was to be joined to his wife—not his girlfriend, not his significant other, not even his fiancée.

Unfortunately, sexual intimacy in our culture has also become casual. Even junior high, high school and college students have now redefined sexual relationships, believing that any form of sexual expression apart from genital penetration is not in reality sex. Sadly, this kind of distorted thinking and rationalization was popularized in the highest office of the land. Today, we must ask another question: Whatever happened to Jesus' teaching when He said,

You have heard that it was said, "Do not commit adultery." But I tell you that anyone who looks at a woman lustfully has already committed adultery with her in his heart (Matt. 5:27-28).

2. Marital intimacy—*Intimate sexual relationships within a legitimate marriage are to be an integral part of that relationship.*
When either marriage partner selfishly refuses to meet the sexual needs of the other partner, that person is violating God's will. Paul made this point clear in his first letter to the Corinthians:

The husband should fulfill his marital duty to his wife, and likewise the wife to her husband. The wife's body does not belong to her alone but also to her husband. In the same way, the husband's body does not belong to him alone but also to his wife. Do not deprive each other except by mutual consent and for a time, so that you may devote yourselves to prayer. Then come together again so that Satan will not tempt you because of your lack of self-control (7:3-5).

It should be noted that there are other instructions in Scripture that add additional perspective to the above guideline. For example, relationships between Christian husbands and wives are to be governed by an attitude of unselfishness, humility and self-sacrifice (see Eph. 5:22-23). This is important because some individuals use Paul's statements to the Corinthians as a reason to make excessive demands on a marriage partner that are definitely out of harmony with the spirit of love that reflects Jesus Christ.

3. God's purpose—*Sexual intimacy is designed by God in a marriage relationship to be more than a means of procreation.*

God designed this relationship to be pleasurable and fun and a means of meeting physical and psychological needs. It's also the ultimate expression of love, concern and unity between a husband and a wife.

4. Form and freedom—*God designed sexual relationships to be the most creative experiences a husband and wife can have together.*

The Bible sets no restrictions on the way sex is expressed in a marriage relationship. However, it is always to be a mutual expression of Christlike love and should be pleasant and fulfilling for both parties.

5. Pure motives—*God has definitely given a woman sexual power over a man.*

A wife's unique physical beauty, her feminine charms, her ability to give and receive physical pleasure and her capacity to provide emotional security—all of these gifts should be used by her to their fullest capacity in order to help her husband be a fulfilled person.

On the other hand, these sexual powers are to be definitely restricted and used exclusively in relationship to her husband. With all other men, she is to be discreet and modest. In no way should she deliberately or even naively attract men to herself sexually. To do so is to violate Paul's instructions to be pure.

Thinking and Growing Together

The following questions are designed for group discussion after reading and studying the content of the chapter:

- How do Paul's instructions in Ephesians 5:3-7 and in 1 Thessalonians 4:1-8 relate to the subject of this chapter?
- What should a Christian woman do if she has lingering guilt over past immoral behavior (see 1 John 1:9)?
- How do Christian women vary in their temptations to be impure and what might explain the variance?
- What would you advise a woman to do if she has negative attitudes toward her sexual relationship with her husband?
- About what can the group pray for you personally?

Set a Goal

Write out one goal you would like to achieve as a result of this study.

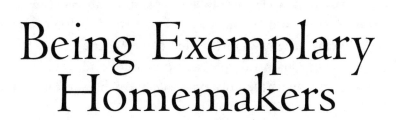

CHAPTER 10

Being Exemplary Homemakers

To be busy at home
TITUS 2:5

A Biblical Portrait of Mary and Martha, Two Special Homemakers

Jesus had no permanent dwelling place. But there was one very special location where He always felt welcome: the home of two sisters named Mary and Martha and their brother, Lazarus. Jesus loved to spend time with these three special friends who lived in Bethany. Clearly, a major factor was that Mary and Martha were wonderful homemakers. While Jesus would share His heart with Lazarus, perhaps lounging in a quiet corner, these two women would busily prepare a delicious meal—something Jesus probably seldom had because of His nomadic lifestyle and ministry.

The Pain of Death

When Lazarus became seriously ill, these devoted sisters sent word to Jesus and asked Him to come, knowing He could heal their brother and His beloved friend. But Jesus purposely waited until Lazarus died. In fact, He had told His disciples that He was glad that He had waited until Lazarus had died (see John 11:15). The reason for this is clearly so He could raise Lazarus from the dead and demonstrate that He was "the resurrection and the life" (v. 25).

When Jesus finally arrived on the scene, His humanness is once again evident. He deeply "loved Martha and her sister and Lazarus" (v. 5), and He was very sad that His dear friends were experiencing the pain of losing a loved one. When He saw Mary's tears of pain, "he was deeply moved in spirit and troubled" (v. 33). In fact, this is the only time that the Bible indicates that "Jesus wept" (v. 35).

A Warm, Inviting Environment

We cannot separate Jesus' sadness and emotional pain from His memories of visiting in this home. Mary and Martha always created an atmosphere that made Him feel welcome.

Evidently, this family was not only well-to-do but also very generous. After all, Mary anointed Jesus' feet with "a pint of pure nard, an expensive perfume" (12:3), which, assuming Judas was not exaggerating, "was worth a year's wages" (12:5).

Though it may appear that Mary was more concerned than Martha about visiting with Jesus and sitting as His feet in order to learn, they both were very dedicated to their Lord and each in her own way served Him faithfully. True, on one occasion, Martha was quite upset that Mary was spending time with Jesus while she was busy preparing a meal. In fact, Martha complained, but the Savior calmed her spirit by helping her understand what her priorities ought to be at that moment (see Luke 10:38-42). From this incident, however, we certainly cannot conclude that Mary was more spiritual than Martha. Together they created a wonderful and hospitable atmosphere. They were indeed good homemakers.

A Woman's Reflections

It's a privilege to introduce you to Joyce Saffel, who serves alongside her husband, Dwight, an elder at Fellowship Bible Church North.

Dear Reader,

As I read the biblical portrait of Mary and Martha as well as the rest of this chapter, one person came to mind: my maternal grandmother. She was a model for me in my growing up years in Southern Illinois.

Unfortunately, my grandfather was killed in a mine explosion, making my grandmother a very young widow. Understandably, she had to work to support her young family, which included my mother who was 12 years old at the time. Being creative, my grandmother decided to open her home to boarders so that she could stay home with her children.

Grandma's day started very early and often went late into the night as she cared for her household. The boarders all called her "Misses," and they helped around the house and in the garden. They loved and respected her and her family.

Eventually, my mother grew up and married, and I came along. I often spent summers with Grandma, and since I was a captive audience, she taught me to cook, to clean house and especially to be hospitable to the people in her home.

As I grew older, I had one goal in life: to be a homemaker. I wanted to get married, have children and be able to stay home with them as Grandma had done. Thankfully, God gave me the desire of my heart. Today I have a loving husband and four wonderful children, who are now married to Christian spouses and are busy in their own homes.

As the years passed by and college expenses came, I had no choice but to work outside the home. But my main concern was to always be home when my children were there. My goal was to work my schedule around theirs, as well as my husband's.

In recent years, since my children are now grown, I have retired from steady outside employment and have served in a ministry to young mothers in our church. I love to interact with these young women, encouraging them to love the Lord and their mates and to be proud to be a mother. I encourage them to lead their children to a saving knowledge of the Lord Jesus Christ and to pray that they will grow up to choose godly mates and to create their own Christ-centered homes.

This is my prayer for you as well, dear reader, for when Christ is at the center of your home, it will be a place where people want to be.

In His Name,
Joyce Saffel

First Things First

It's very clear then that when Paul wrote to Titus and instructed him to teach the older women so that they in turn could train the younger women to be busy at home, he was addressing a woman's priorities. In the New Testament culture particularly, a woman found it difficult to function productively and spiritually outside the context of family life. She had very little to do other than to gossip and to get into difficulties, particularly moral difficulties. Consequently, Paul advised these young women to marry or, if they were married, to avoid being busy in places other than within their homes.

Paul addressed this issue when he wrote to Timothy in Ephesus. Many young widows had developed "the habit of being idle and going about from house to house" (1 Tim. 5:13). In the process, they were tempted not only to "become idlers, but also gossips and busybodies, saying things they ought not to" (v. 13). Consequently, Paul counseled these young women "to marry, to have children, to *manage their homes* and to give the enemy no opportunity for slander" (v. 14).

The need Paul was addressing in Crete was more than cultural however. But before we look at the supracultural aspects of this qualification for maturity, let's look specifically at what Paul was *not* teaching.

1. Paul was not teaching that a woman couldn't be active outside the home, even pursuing a professional career.

Consider Proverbs 31:10-31. In this passage, in addition to the many home responsibilities, an excellent wife is presented as a woman who is involved in real-estate investments (see v. 16) and who has her own manufacturing business (see v. 24).

In the New Testament era, Lydia stands out as a wonderful example of the Proverbs 31 woman. We meet her in Philippi.

Clearly, she was not only a good manager of her own household but also a very successful businesswoman, "a dealer in purple cloth" (Acts 16:14). She was originally from Thyatira, a city noted for its dyeing industry and the production of purple garments, which were highly prized and costly.

Apparently, Lydia was a Gentile but was a convert to Judaism. When she first heard the gospel, she was attending a prayer meeting on the bank of the river that flowed through Philippi. It was there that she heard the gospel message from Paul and his missionary team and put her faith in Christ for salvation. She then introduced these men to her whole household, which included both her children and her servants. Lydia's entire extended family responded to the gospel and demonstrated their faith through water baptism (see Acts 16:15).

Pertinent to our discussion, Lydia not only managed a large household but also was very successful in business. We know nothing of her husband, who may have died or may have been killed in one of the Roman wars. Evidently, the growing church in Philippi first met in Lydia's home. She used her resources to serve, not only Paul and his missionary team, but also the whole church. She was a generous woman and no doubt encouraged the Philippian believers to support Paul financially as he continued his missionary ministry (see Phil. 4:15-16).

2. Paul was not teaching that a wife and mother must do all of the work in the home by herself.

Unfortunately, there are some Christian husbands and fathers who will never lift a finger to help with the housework because they believe it is the wife's God-ordained responsibility. There is nothing in the Bible to support this kind of interpretation. It reflects subjective reasoning and makes the Bible teach something it does not teach. In fact, the Bible teaches that a Christian husband is to love his wife as Christ loved the Church, which means demonstrating an attitude of unselfishness, humility and sensitivity (see Phil. 2:5-8; 1 Pet. 3:7). In essence, a godly husband and father has a servant's heart.

Some Christians extend this erroneous concept to include never allowing their wives to secure outside help with the housework. This, of course, runs counter to biblical illustrations because many wives in both the Old Testament and the New Testament had servants to help them with their responsibilities. In fact, the woman described in Proverbs 31 had a number of servants and helpers.

Obviously, to apply this principle today is dependent on the family's financial resources as well as other social dynamics. For example, both of us grew up in farming communities. Our parents were anything but wealthy. In fact, they were barely able to make ends meet. However, we always had plenty of good food on the table and clothes to wear.

There is nothing in the Bible that says Christian husbands and fathers should never lift a finger to help with the housework because it is the wife's God-ordained responsibility.

I (Gene) remember those days well. When I was only six years old, Aunt Ida, my mother's unmarried sister, came to live with us in order to help mom with all of the household chores. She cooked meals for 10 hungry people (my grandfather lived with us as well) and washed all of our clothes. She was always busy cleaning the house. It was a huge responsibility.

Needless to say, Aunt Ida became an integral part of the family, since she lived in our home until she needed special care in a nursing home. When that time came, all of us children, who were grown by then, made sure that she had wonderful care until she went home to be with the Lord at age 90.

Aunt Ida's service in our home enabled my mother to fill a much broader role: to help manage the family farm. Though my mother often assisted with the housework, she spent much of her time outdoors managing a rather large chicken business. Dad's time was spent farming the land, milking cows and operating a milk route (picking up milk from other farms and delivering it to the local dairy).

This kind of social dynamic is rare in our culture today, but it illustrates the creative ways this principle of being busy at home is applied in various social situations at various moments in history.

3. Paul was not teaching that being busy at home indicates that women have an inferior position to men, who are busy outside the home.

In Jesus Christ, we are all equal. Paul made this clear when he wrote, "There is neither Jew nor Greek, slave nor free, *male nor female*, for you are *all one* in Christ Jesus" (Gal. 3:28). In God's sight, a woman's spiritual position in Christ and a man's are no different. In fact, they are as one. There are no distinctions based on gender. However, as we'll discuss in the final chapter of this book, God has established some temporal and functional roles for women, especially because of the principle of sin that is operative in the world. But this in no way makes them second-class citizens.

In essence, being a homemaker is not a menial task that is second in importance to being the breadwinner. Furthermore, as we've already noted, this God-ordained role need not restrict her in accomplishing other tasks outside the home. Some of the greatest literary, artistic and scientific achievements have been accomplished by women. Being busy at home in no way need stand in the way of demonstrating a woman's creative potential.

A Matter of Priorities

As stated earlier, Paul's reference to being busy at home is based on more than cultural considerations. When a woman chooses to be a wife and mother, she has chosen a definite God-ordained role. Since the beginning of creation, and particularly after the Fall, God's plan is that a married woman's priority is to be in her home. Her husband's priority is to be the provider. God confirmed this arrangement after the Fall when He said that Eve would bear children and that by the sweat of his face, Adam was to provide for his family (see Gen. 3:16-19). The priorities are God-ordained.

Therefore, a married woman who wants to be in the will of God will make her home a priority. Even though God certainly allows a great deal of freedom as to how she carries out her responsibilities, she is to develop a plan to maintain this priority. If she does not, her marriage and family life are headed for serious problems. She cannot violate a biblical principle without suffering serious consequences.

A Personal Story

As a mother, I (Elaine) had the unique opportunity of not having to work outside the home after our children were born. Even though there were months and years when we found it very difficult to make ends meet, I was determined to make our home a priority. In fact, living on one income taught both of us not only to establish priorities but also to walk by faith.

Early in our marriage, we also determined to tithe (give 10 percent of our income to the Lord's work). In order to maintain this commitment, we determined to spend money only on things we needed, not on things we wanted. Even then, there were times when we ran out of money before the next payday.

I remember one experience particularly. I was ironing clothes that day and wondering where we were going to get money to buy formula for our little girl. We had literally run out of money. Fearful but prayerful, I committed the matter to the Lord.

And then it happened! That day we received a small check in the mail from the local department store, an amount that we unknowingly had overpaid when we purchased our lawnmower. In fact, it was just enough to buy formula for our baby girl! Needless to say, we were thankful, and we were able to meet our needs until the next payday.

Though these were challenging years, we would not have done things differently. I was able to devote time to our children. We both believe that providing them with my consistent presence in their lives was more important than the things we could have bought for them and ourselves during those start-up years. When we look back, we are absolutely certain that God honored this priority.

We both realize, of course, that this arrangement may not be possible for some young couples. On the other hand, we believe a lot of people are unable to make the decision to stay at home with their children because they are caught up in a materialistic world. To be perfectly honest, years went by before we were able to purchase the furniture and other amenities we would have loved to have had in our first home. However, when we look at the result of waiting, the wait was worth it! Eventually we were able to get some things we desired in addition to the things our family needed to live.

Singleness and Fulfillment

The Bible clearly teaches that singleness need not interfere with the sense of fulfillment that can come with rearing a family. It's true that single women who are living in a marriage-conscious society may feel cheated. It's possible that they will fall into the trap of introspection and loneliness, which in turn can lead to anxiety and even bitterness. Fortunately our culture provides single women with many opportunities for fulfillment in other meaningful ways.

One outstanding illustration of a single woman called by God to a life of fruitful service is the late Dr. Henrietta Mears. Of her, Dr. Billy Graham once said: "She has had a remarkable influence, both directly and indirectly, on my life. In fact, I doubt if any other woman outside of my wife and mother has had such a marked influence . . . she is certainly one of the greatest Christians I've ever known."[1]

Dr. Mears's influence was also significant in the life of Bill Bright, founder of Campus Crusade for Christ. Bill was a member of the college group she taught, and it was in her home that Campus Crusade was launched. Only eternity will tell how many people have put their faith in Jesus Christ as a result of Campus Crusade's dynamic ministry.

Under Dr. Mears's leadership as Director of Christian Education at the Hollywood Presbyterian Church, Sunday School enrollment grew from 450 to 4,200 in two and a half years—an average weekly gain of over 30 people per Sunday. Out of the college class that she taught, hundreds of young men and women were challenged to go into the ministry. Furthermore, the Gospel Light Sunday School literature written by Dr. Mears and her coworkers at the church became material that now circles the globe. In fact, *The Measure of a Woman* is published by Regal Books, a division of Gospel Light Publications.

But this outstanding and fruitful life was not without a period of crisis in her younger days. She had many male friends but really loved only one, a man of a different faith. When faced with tension and conflict about this decision, she turned to the Lord and prayed,

> Lord, you have made me the way I am. I love a home, I love security, I love children, and I love him. Yet I feel that marriage under these conditions would draw me away from you. I surrender even this, Lord, and leave it in your hands. Lead me, Lord, and strengthen me. You have promised to fulfill all my needs. I trust in you alone.[2]

After this prayer, the friendship was ended. Many years later as she looked back on this experience, Dr. Mears wrote:

> The marvelous thing has been, that the Lord has always given me a beautiful home; he has given me thousands of children; he has supplied every need in my life, and I've never felt lonely. Since I am a very gregarious person, I thought I would have a feeling I didn't belong. But I've never had it, never! I've never missed companionship. Through one experience after another the Lord has shown me that he had something special for me to do. After I went through that final door, where it was just the Lord and I, into wide open spaces of people and things and excitement, life has been one great adventure.[3]

This does not mean that every unmarried Christian girl need experience the success of Dr. Mears to feel significant. A human being can discover fulfillment in many fulfilling relationships or in just a few. The important thing is that a young single woman must break the shackles of the cultural conditioning that tells her that the only route to happiness is marriage (or some other form of sexual intimacy with the opposite sex).

Though God ordained marriage and family as a major means for fulfillment, it is not the only way. There are other avenues available for the woman who gains a proper perspective on life and eternal values. Most important, she must realize that Jesus Christ is her constant companion. Furthermore, being a member of the loving, functioning Body of Christ—the family of God—can provide rich and fulfilling relationships.

Though God ordained marriage and family as a major means for fulfillment, it is not the only way.

Thinking and Growing Together

The following questions are designed for group discussion after reading and studying the content of this chapter:

- How can a married woman with children at home evaluate whether she is maintaining proper biblical priorities?
- Why is it often difficult, particularly in our society, for some mothers with children at home to experience fulfillment?
- Why is Paul's instruction for young mothers to be busy at home a controversial exhortation among some women—

even among Christian women?
- Why are some women able to be good mothers and be involved in a number of activities outside of the home while other women cannot?
- About what can the group pray for you personally?

Set a Goal

Write out one goal you would like to achieve as a result of this study.

CHAPTER 11

Doing Good Works

To be kind
TITUS 2:5

A Biblical Portrait of Dorcas, Who Was Always Doing Good

How would you like to have the following epitaph engraved on your tombstone?

She always did good and helped the poor!

This is the way Dorcas was described by those who knew her (see Acts 9:36). She lived in Joppa, a city now identified as Tel Aviv in modern Israel. Whether married or single, she devoted much of her time creating beautiful robes and other clothing for the poor. She was a generous and benevolent woman.

For some unstated reason, Dorcas became ill and died. Her friends washed her body and placed her in an upstairs room, as deep feelings of grief spread throughout the city and beyond.

Then it happened! Word got around that Peter was in Lydda, a town about 10 miles southeast of Joppa. With the power of Jesus Christ, he had miraculously healed a paralytic who had been bedridden for eight years. Two men traveled immediately to Lydda and begged Peter to come to Joppa. Perhaps he could also help Dorcas—even though she had died.

Peter agreed to go:

Peter went with them, and when he arrived he was taken upstairs to the room. All the widows stood around him, crying and showing him the robes and other clothing that Dorcas had made while she was still with them (Acts 9:39).

What began as a very sad story ended with great excitement, rejoicing and conversions to Jesus Christ. Peter, in the power of the Holy Spirit, raised Dorcas from the dead, and consequently, "many people believed in the Lord" (Acts 9:42).

The primary reason Luke recorded this miracle in the book of Acts was to report on the number of people who put their faith in Christ. Miracles were basically designed by God in those early years to confirm the message of salvation (see Heb. 2:2-4). But there's another important truth that stands out in bold relief in this story: Dorcas was a woman who illustrates beautifully what Paul had in mind when he instructed older women to teach the younger women to be kind.

Dorcas's good deeds involved helping the poor. The widows who gathered to mourn her death held in their hands the clothes that Dorcas had made while she was still with them. She was a kind and generous woman who used her skills to meet the needs of others.

Interestingly, the Greek name "Dorcas," as well as the Aramaic equivalent "Tabitha," means "a gazelle," which is an emblem of beauty.[1] Relative to this symbolism, Lange comments:

> The gazelle is distinguished for its slender and beautiful form, its graceful movements and its soft but brilliant eyes; it is frequently introduced by the Hebrews and other Oriental nations as an image of female loveliness, and the name was often employed as a proper name, in the case of females.[2]

We're not told whether or not Dorcas was beautiful in a physical sense. However, it's clear from the biblical story that she was beautiful on the inside. As Herbert Lockyer states: "She certainly lived a lovely life, and had eyes reflecting the compassion of the Master whom she so faithfully served. All whom she influenced and helped saw in her the beauty of Jesus."[3]

A Woman's Reflections

It's a privilege to introduce you to Barbara Debenport, who serves along with her husband, Dan, an elder at Fellowship Bible Church North.

Dear Reader,

Prior to becoming a Christian, I always tried to live by two principles: Never say anything bad to anyone, and treat others as I want to be treated. When I became a Christian, I was amazed to learn that the two greatest commandments Jesus taught were to love God with all our hearts and to love our neighbors as ourselves (see Matt. 22:37-39).

Every day I must choose how I will treat the people I encounter. So do you! Because of the Holy Spirit's presence in my life, I have access to His fruit, which includes love, joy, peace, patience, kindness, goodness, faithfulness, gentleness and self-control (see Gal. 5:22-23). I can think and act like the sinner I am or live by the Holy Spirit's power and exhibit Christ's likeness—which certainly includes goodness and kindness.

In order to develop the quality of kindness, I have set the following goals:

- *To pray for a change of heart in order to be kind toward others—especially toward the people who get under my skin.*
- *To look for opportunities to do random acts of kindness to strangers or people in need. For example, I've given a hot cup of coffee to a school crossing guard on a cold morning. I've shared a bag of food with a homeless person. I've given a rose to a stranger and sent a note of encouragement to cheer someone up.*
- *To write on my calendar key dates, or happenings, in the lives of my friends and then follow up with a phone call to see how things turn out. This is especially meaningful when they have doctor's appointments.*
- *To seek out a lonely person to be a friend.*

I'm sure you can add to these examples from your own life. When you think about it, the opportunities to show kindness are endless.

My prayer for you is that you would choose to live for God daily in order to grow in His Spirit and to display God's love and kindness to all those you encounter.

Because of His kindness toward me,
Barbara Debenport

Excelling in Goodness

The Greek word *agathos,* which Luke used to describe Dorcas and which Paul also used to describe a mature Christian woman in his letter to Titus, means to excel in any respect, to be distinguished, to be good, to be kind.[4] It's used to describe not only people but also things, conditions, deeds, times and seasons. When it's used to describe people, the word is sometimes used in a narrower sense—a person who is benevolent, kind or generous. This explains why the translators of the *New International Version* used the word "kind" to convey the meaning of "agathos."[5]

Another Biblical Perspective

In his first letter to Timothy, Paul described in more detail what he had in mind when he instructed older women to teach younger women to be good, or kind. In this letter, Paul was dealing with widows who were *truly* widows: They had no children or grandchildren to help care for their daily needs. Paul proceeded to set forth specific criteria for evaluating a woman who was eligible for material assistance:

No widow may be put on the list of widows [that is, to be cared for by the church] unless she is over sixty, has been faithful to her husband, and is *well known for her good deeds*, such as bringing up children, showing hospitality, washing the feet of the saints, helping those in trouble and devoting herself to *all kinds of good deeds* (1 Tim. 5:9-10).

Paul then described what he meant by "all kinds of good deeds." At the top of his list was "bringing up children." What kind of mother was she? Did she consider child rearing her primary responsibility in the home?

Paul next spoke of "showing hospitality." How did this woman use her home? Did she share it with others? Was she unselfish with her own material blessings?

Paul also listed "washing the feet of the saints" as being a good deed. Open sandals and dusty roads created obvious difficulties. Consequently, it was a common practice for a host to wash a visitor's feet, which became a means of showing hospitality and of demonstrating humility. Jesus Christ dramatically modeled these qualities when He stooped to wash His disciples' feet in the Upper Room (see John 13:14-15). His act was the ultimate in servanthood.

Paul next stated that these good deeds involved "helping those in trouble." Obviously, this was an open-ended gesture. It could have included any kind of difficulty and almost any kind of assistance. It may have ranged from sharing a cup of cold water to being a good Samaritan to someone who was in serious trouble.

Paul ended the list by stating that a mature Christian woman devoted herself to "all kinds of good deeds." With this remark, Paul was demonstrating that what he had just listed as good deeds were merely introductory comments that illustrated what could and should be done. What may have been good deeds in one situation may not have been relevant in another. And furthermore, what may have been a good deed in the first-century culture—such as washing the feet of saints—may no longer be necessary in our twenty-first-century culture. In any case, in every culture of the world, there are many ways to be devoted to doing good deeds. In his letter to Titus, Paul certainly implied that a woman who was, and is, maturing in her Christian faith would be the kind of woman who did good deeds.

Two Women Who Marked Our Lives

Two people immediately come to mind when we think of women who did good deeds in our lives. Although they were parts of our lives many years ago, the impact that they had remains to this day.

A Sunday School Teacher

I (Elaine) remember an experience when I was about five years old. My family went to visit my Sunday School teacher, who lived with her elderly parents. I can still visualize the setting, but what I remember the most is how kindly and respectfully my teacher treated her parents. "Father," she would say, "let me help you to the table." Then she would carefully assist him as he made his way cautiously across the room. "Mother," she would ask, "can I get you something?"

I remember not only these actions but also my teacher's voice—its tenderness and softness that reflected concern. I also recollect emulating her behavior. When I was still a preschooler, my grandmother came to live with my family for a while when my grandmother was ill. She stayed in an upstairs room in the family's farmhouse. I remember clearly telling her that if she needed anything, to be sure to tap her cane on the floor and I'd bring her what she needed.

As women, either older or younger, modeling kindness is a powerful means to communicate how to live a Christlike life. This is certainly what Paul had in mind when he told Titus to train the younger women to be busy at home and to be kind.

A First-Grade Teacher

I (Gene) remember a woman who touched my life in a dramatic way—so much so that I'll never forget what happened as long as I live. I was only six years old and enrolled in the first grade. My teacher's name was Miss Olive Owens, a name that is also indelibly impressed on my mind.

After seeing my pitiful attempts at writing, my first-grade teacher quietly whispered in my ear, "That's alright, Gene."

At some point, Miss Owens went to the chalkboard and, in what I've now come to know as beautiful cursive, wrote the word "me." At that moment in my life, I had never seen the word either printed or in cursive. Those were pre-Sesame Street days. She then asked each of us to copy the word on our writing pads.

I remember looking at the chalkboard and then at my paper. Try as I might, I couldn't get my pencil to cooperate. As I looked at the word as Miss Owens had written it and compared it with what I was trying to put on my paper, I began to panic. Though I was only six years old, I could tell that I wasn't even coming close to making a good copy.

My anxiety increased when Miss Owens began to walk down each row, looking at each student's paper. I noticed that she would compliment each of my classmates. As she stopped at the desk just in front of me, my heart began to pound. What would she think? What would she say?

And then there she was, standing beside me and looking at my paper. Fear overwhelmed me and I burst into tears. It didn't take her long to discern what was happening. I'll never forget what she did. After looking at my paper and seeing my pitiful efforts at writing, she bent over and quietly whispered in my ear, "That's alright, Gene." She then kissed me gently on the cheek and went on to the next student.

You can imagine what happened in my little six-year-old heart. I'll never forget the relief. My teacher loved me even though what I had written looked like the result of a runaway seismograph. I'll never forget that moment. Miss Owens's kindness in my life dramatically changed my perspective on school. It very well could have made the difference between my feeling comfortable in an academic setting or feeling insecure for many years to come.

A Broader Biblical Perspective

Throughout Scripture, we're taught as Christians to do good. The following statements and Scriptures are for all believers, which, of course, includes women, the focus of this study.

1. We are to do good to all people—Christians and non-Christians alike.

Let us not become weary in *doing good*, for at the proper time we will reap a harvest if we do not give up. Therefore, as we have opportunity, let us *do good to all people,*

especially to those who belong to the family of believers
(Gal. 6:9-10).

Remind the people to be subject to rulers and authori-
ties, to be obedient, to be ready to *do whatever is good*, to
slander no one, to be peaceable and considerate, and to
show true humility toward all men (Titus 3:1-2).

2. Doing good should be a natural result of our salvation.

For it is by grace you have been saved, through faith—
and this not from yourselves, it is the gift of God—not
by works, so that no one can boast. For we are God's
workmanship, created in Christ Jesus to *do good works*,
which God prepared in advance for us to do (Eph. 2:8-
10).

3. Doing good involves what we say as well as what we do.

Do not let any unwholesome talk come out of your
mouths, but only what is *helpful* [good] for building others up according to their needs, that it may benefit those
who listen (Eph. 4:29).

4. Employee-employer relationships help give us unique opportunities to do good.

Slaves, obey your earthly masters with respect and fear,
and with sincerity of heart, just as you would obey
Christ. Serve wholeheartedly, as if you were serving the
Lord, not men, because you know that the Lord will
reward everyone for whatever *good* he does, whether he is
slave or free (Eph. 6:5,7-8).

5. Our prayer, like Paul's, should be that we will bear fruit in every good work.

> And we pray this in order that you may live a life worthy of the Lord and may please him in every way: *bearing fruit in every good work*, growing in the knowledge of God (Col. 1:10).

6. A Christian should repay evil with good.

> Make sure that nobody pays back wrong for wrong, but always try to be *kind* [good] to each other and to everyone else (1 Thess. 5:15).

> Do not repay evil with evil or insult with insult, but with blessing, because to this you were called so that you may inherit a blessing. For, "Whoever would love life and see good days . . . must turn from evil and *do good*; he must seek peace and pursue it" (1 Pet. 3:9-11).

Thinking and Growing Together

The following questions are designed for group discussion after reading and studying the content of this chapter:

- Reread Ephesians 2:8-10 and discuss the gift of salvation and what should happen once we receive this gift. Why is it so important to distinguish between doing good works as a Christian and doing good works in order to become a Christian?
- Why is the quality of being kind, or doing good, one of the most comprehensive qualities of maturity in Paul's profile in Titus 2:3-5? How does this specific quality relate

to each of the other qualities outlined in these verses?
- How can we use words to demonstrate this quality (see Prov. 12:25; 16:24; 25:11)?
- Share with the other members of your group about a woman who marked your life by being kind or by doing what is good.
- About what can the group pray for you personally?

Set a Goal

Write out one goal you would like to achieve as a result of this study.

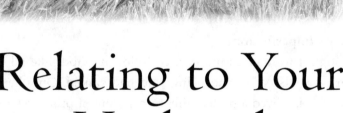

Relating to Your Husband

To be subject to their husbands

TITUS 2:5

A Biblical Portrait of Mary, the Mother of Jesus

No woman in the biblical story from Genesis to Revelation illustrates a submissive spirit more than Mary. Though there are no direct references to this quality of maturity in terms of her relationship with her husband, Joseph, there is a moving illustration in terms of her relationship with God. True, she was greatly puzzled, and rightly so, when the angel Gabriel told her she would "be with child and give birth to a son" (Luke 1:31). But when this heavenly messenger explained the supernatural aspects of her pregnancy, Mary responded, "I am the Lord's servant. . . . May it be to me as you have said" (v. 38).

Even before Mary understood that Jesus would also be her personal Savior and the One who would be the head of the Church, she recognized God the Father as her Lord. We're not told why God chose her for this sacred event, but based on her response to Gabriel as a divine spokesman, Mary already had a deep desire to live in the will of God. We can also assume that this desire to submit to God's will defined her relationship with Joseph as well: She recognized him as her spiritual leader.

Mary's Imperfections

Though a woman committed to following God, like all of us Mary was also a human being who had sinned. Only her son, Jesus Christ, lived a perfect life. In her song of praise, Mary recognized God as her Savior (see Luke 1:47). It is clear, then, that she had sinned, since only sinners need to be saved.

However, in spite of her human weaknesses, she was a young woman with an unusual inner beauty. Herbert Lockyer captures this reality:

> As we read the narrative given by Luke, to whom, as a physician, Mary could speak intimately of her profound experience, we are impressed with her quietness of spirit, meditative inwardness of disposition, admirable self-control, devout and gracious gift of sacred silence, and a mind saturated with the spirit and promises of the Old Testament.[1]

Mary's Humility

We see the quality of submission in Mary's life both in her response to God's word through Gabriel and throughout her life. Imagine the scene at the cross, as she stood silently in over-whelming grief. Donald Davidson envisions the thought that may have pierced her heart:

> In that moment the tremendous truth must at last have dawned upon Mary, that He who hung upon the cross was not her son; that before the world was He was; that so far from being His mother, she was herself His child.[2]

We catch a final glimpse of Mary's humility in the Upper Room following Christ's ascension. Meeting with the apostles, she is mentioned, not first in the list, but last, along with a general reference to Jesus' brothers (see Acts 1:13-14). There is no evidence whatsoever of any jealousy or desire on Mary's part to be honored or even recognized as the one who gave birth to the God-man. She quietly took her place as a submissive follower of those whom Jesus had chosen to launch the Church, of which she was now a part. Like all of us, she was a sinner saved by God's grace.

The major lesson we can learn from Mary's example is that for any Christian woman, biblical submission to her husband begins with her submission to God. This is why Paul wrote to the Ephesians: "Wives, submit to your husbands *as to the Lord*" (Eph. 5:22). Normally, a woman who is fully following Christ Jesus finds it much easier to submit to her husband. Conversely, a woman who has not presented her body to Jesus Christ as a living sacrifice and who is allowing herself to be conformed to this world will also struggle in her relationship with her husband (see Rom. 12:1-2).

A Woman's Reflections

It's a privilege to introduce you to Joan Craig, who serves along with her husband, John, an elder at Fellowship Bible Church North.

Dear Reader,

If I could leave one legacy to my daughters and other young women, it would be the importance of loving and supporting your husband. God gave him to you for a reason—to deeply love him, to be your partner in life and to experience all that God has for both of you. Sometimes we all get so busy and sidetracked that we forget God's purpose for our lives. As wives, we are to be help-mates, or complements, to our husbands, and we are to encourage them to take the leadership by respecting and submitting to them. Yes, I did use that word: "submit."

As I pen this letter, my husband and I are celebrating our forty-fourth wedding anniversary. As I look back, I can certainly say that both of us have made mistakes in our marriage (just ask our children). We've both been blessed with high energy and discipline. However, we're also strong-willed. This can be a bad combination.

But even before I became a Christian and even knew the word "submit," I was committed to supporting my husband in whatever way possible. Since my husband traveled a lot and we had three children, I realized early on that it was very important for me to maintain an organized household. I also attempted to help him further his career by being his sounding board, entertaining business-people in our home and keeping myself physically attractive.

However, there were many times I failed to reach my goals because I allowed my strong-willed nature to challenge him. On the other hand, these rather tense moments gave us the opportu-

nity to grow in our relationship: to express our views in non-threatening ways.

I must say that I have been blessed with a wonderful husband who seeks to love God and who truly loves me. This has made it easier for me to submit to his authority. I believe that because of John's love and support, God requires more from me, since "to whom much is given, from him much will be required" (Luke 12:48, NKJV).

Both Paul and Peter made it clear that submission is a unique part of our calling as Christian wives. Christ, of course, is the supreme illustration of this truth, and we are to follow in His steps (see 1 Pet. 2:21). Ultimately, we will reap the benefits. One of those benefits in my family has been the spiritual leadership that my husband has taken, and I'm thrilled to see our son following in his father's footsteps.

Serving Him,
Joan Craig

The Cultural Setting

Imagine for a moment what it was like for a married woman to live on the island of Crete. Though the Romans generally "were much more ready than Greeks to admit that women could make a valuable contribution to the proper functioning of society,"[3] they were often "only allowed to say what men wanted to hear from them."[4] In terms of marriage and male authority, particularly in the early Roman Empire, Otto Kiefer commented:

We must not forget that the husband could commit no action which the law recognized as a breach of his marriage-tie; he had an entirely free hand. And the liberty of wives was so restricted that they seldom had the opportunity to commit misconduct—especially since they were faced with terrifying punishments if they were convicted. Her punishment was not only to be driven with disgrace and infamy from the home in which she had lived, as well as that, she could be put to death by the family council in co-operation with the husband.[5]

Though this is a description of marriage in ancient Rome, knowing what we do about the Cretan culture, we can certainly conclude that much remained the same in terms of how husbands viewed their wives.

But also imagine what happened when the gospel penetrated this culture. Paul brought a message of hope and freedom that these women had never heard or experienced before. We can be certain that Paul shared the same good news that he had written to the Galatians years earlier:

You are all sons [and daughters] of God through faith in Christ Jesus, for all of you who were baptized into Christ have clothed yourselves with Christ. There is neither Jew nor Greek, slave nor free, *male nor female*, for you are all one in Christ Jesus (3:26-28).

Considering the bondage that permeated the lives of these women, they would have interpreted and applied Paul's words very personally to their own plight. Not surprisingly, many would be tempted to overreact to this new freedom in Christ.

Paul, then, was obviously writing to Titus to help him correct a problem, particularly among young married women in Crete. However, we believe the issue of wifely submission is more than a cultural concern. It is also based on a supracultural principle that grows out of the whole of the biblical story.

Wifely Submission

The Bible *does* teach that wives should submit to their husbands. In addition to his instructions in his letter to Titus, without equivocation Paul wrote to the Ephesians and Colossians: "Wives, *submit* to your husbands" (Eph. 5:22; Col. 3:18). And to make sure the Ephesian Christians really understood what he said, he added,

> For the husband is the *head of the wife* as Christ is the head of the church, his body, of which he is the Savior. Now as the church *submits to Christ*, so also wives *should submit to their husbands* in everything (5:23-24).[6]

Peter too emphasized that women should exhibit this same kind of behavior particularly toward non-Christian husbands: "Wives, in the same way be *submissive* to your husbands so that, if any of them do not believe the word, they may be won over without words by the behavior of their wives" (1 Pet. 3:1).

Mutual Submission

Though Paul and Peter taught that wives should indeed submit to their husbands, they also taught that a submissive attitude should characterize all of us in our relationships with each other, regardless of our God-ordained position of authority. Thus, before Paul exhorted wives to be submissive to their husbands, he first exhorted all believers to "*submit to one another* out of reverence for Christ" (Eph. 5:21).

It's interesting that Paul did not use the word translated as "submit" in his statement to wives, although it's included in the English text. Rather, Paul based his directive for wives to submit on his use of the word in verse 21, when he was speaking to all the followers of Christ in Ephesus. In other words, Paul told all of these people to "submit to one another out of reverence for Christ," including wives to husbands (see v. 22), husbands to wives (see v. 25), children to parents (see 6:1), fathers to children (see v. 4), servants to masters (see v. 5) and masters to servants (see v. 9). Put another way, Paul's statement for all believers to submit to one another is the basic concept on which he builds his specific exhortations to all believers mentioned in the remaining part of his Ephesian letter.

Submit to one another out of reverence for Christ.

EPHESIANS 5:21

Servant Leadership

That Paul believed husbands should submit to their wives is clearly implied in the fact that he wrote, "Husbands, love your wives, just as Christ loved the church and *gave himself up for her*" (Eph. 5:25). Jesus demonstrated His love as the Lord of the universe by becoming a servant, and it's impossible to be a servant without being submissive. Consider again His willingness to wash His disciples' feet. Following that dramatic event in the Upper Room, the apostle John recorded what happened:

"Do you understand what I have done for you?" he asked them. "You call me 'Teacher' and 'Lord,' and rightly so, for that is what I am. Now that I, your Lord and Teacher, have washed your feet, you also should wash one another's feet" (John 13:12-14).

In his letter to the Philippians, Paul captured the essence of what Jesus was both modeling and teaching the apostles that day. However, he applied this great truth to all believers, which includes both husbands and wives in their marital relationships:

Do nothing out of selfish ambition or vain conceit, but in humility consider others better than yourselves. Each of you should look not only to your own interests, but also to the interests of others. Your attitude should be the same as that of Christ Jesus: Who, being in very nature God, did not consider equality with God something to be grasped, but made himself nothing, taking the very nature of a servant, being made in human likeness. And being found in appearance as a man, he humbled himself and became obedient to death—even death on a cross! (2:3-8).

A Broader Perspective

To understand the concept of submission for all Christians and for wives in particular, we need to look at the total biblical story.

The Scene in Eden

In Paul's first letter to Timothy, we see that "Adam was formed first, then Eve" (2:13). She was created to come alongside Adam to be his helper (see Gen. 2:18). This does not mean that Eve was inferior to Adam. There's no indication of inequality whatsoever in the original creation story. They were both created in the image of God, reflecting the creator's perfection (see Gen. 1:27). However, even though they worked together to rule over the animal creation, Adam was given from the beginning servant-leadership responsibility in this relationship.

In his letter to Timothy, Paul also stated that a woman should not have authority over a man because it was Eve, not Adam, who was deceived (see 1 Tim. 2:14). Consequently, Eve and all her sisters throughout history have suffered the consequences (see Gen. 3:16).

Does Paul's second reason—that Eve was first deceived and not Adam—mean that all women thereafter would be more prone to deception? We believe the answer is no. What happened to Eve brought *leadership consequences* that are ongoing, not a greater tendency toward deception than that of men. In fact, empirical studies demonstrate that gender is not an issue in a tendency toward deception.[7] And when I (Gene) evaluate my own years of leadership both in my home and in the ministry, I must admit that at times I have been more prone to being deceived than my wife. In fact, I can think of instances when if I had listened to her perspective, I wouldn't have made certain errors in judgment.

Restoration in Jesus Christ

With the coming of Jesus Christ, something very unique happened regarding a woman's role. Husbands and wives who are born again and have both presented themselves to Christ as a living sacrifice and are being transformed into Christ's image (see Rom. 12:1-2) have the potential to experience a significant restoration to the relationship that existed between Adam and Eve in Eden prior to sin's entering the world. In Christ, they can experience unity and oneness that can grow deeper and more meaningful day by day. From God's eternal and spiritual perspective, there is total equality in the relationship—as we see in Paul's letter to the Galatians (see 3:26-28).

On the other hand, since marriage is a human relationship that is affected by the presence of sin in the world, God designed that the husband be the Christlike leader in his home (just as Christ is the head of the Church) and that the woman recognize his God-given authority. However, in this restored relationship, when a husband follows Christ's example, he can submit to his wife without giving up his God-ordained headship and authority. And when a wife loves her husband as Christ loved her, she can submit to her husband without giving up her strategic position as his partner for life.

This, of course, represents God's perfect will, the ideal. Peter acknowledged that not all marriage relationships are mutual in terms of commitment to Christ and to each other. Consequently, even when a husband fails to be the man God intends him to be, a godly wife can still take the lead in demonstrating the quality of submission—which in many instances becomes the means whereby the husband ultimately begins to love her as Christ loved the Church.

Misinterpretations and Misapplications

To understand what the Bible really teaches about submission, particularly for wives, it's helpful to state what the Bible is *not* teaching.

1. Submission does not mean wives should never express their opinions or feelings.

Based on their definition of biblical authority, some men refuse to let their wives express feelings and frustrations, anxieties and anger. However, nothing could be more biblically inaccurate or devastating to a woman's self-worth and emotional and spiritual health. For any husband to deny his wife this privilege is a direct violation of Peter's exhortation to husbands to treat their wives with respect as heirs in Christ Jesus (see 1 Pet. 3:7). The Christian husband who is not sensitive to his wife, who does not listen to her concerns and who does not identify with her emotional and physical pain, is in direct violation of God's will. Unfortunately, this kind of man often uses the Scriptures to justify his own weak ego and his selfish and egotistical behavior. Furthermore, Peter warned that a husband who does not treat his wife with understanding and respect is in danger of experiencing unanswered prayer (see v. 7).

2. Submission does not justify authoritarianism.

There are some men—even Christian men—who interpret "leadership" as authoritarianism. They shout orders, demand instant obedience and meet opposition with psychological, if not physical, force. This is not leadership! It's childishness and selfishness. It's the opposite of love.

I (Gene) will never forget the conversation I had with a young man on my open line radio program called *Let's Talk!* He was obviously terribly frustrated because his wife had decided to leave him. I asked him what her justification was and he responded very quickly by saying, "She believes I am too authoritarian and controlling." "Are you?" I asked. I'll never forget his response. Referring to Genesis 3:16, he queried, "Doesn't the Bible teach that I am to *rule over her*?"

I quickly responded with the explanation that the Bible teaches that men's ruling of their wives is the *result* of sin. God was not giving husbands a command. Rather, He was stating that because of sin, men would be tempted to control, dominate and even abuse their wives. Sadly, he actually believed he was doing the right thing. More accurately, he was probably rationalizing his desire to be in control of his wife. He had no concept of what it means to love as Christ loved.

3. Submission does not mean that a man should be the sole decision maker in the home.

Although the concept of headship certainly involves authority, it does not imply that the wife is incapable of making decisions; nor does it mean that she should not be included in the process. Women, of course, vary in their desire to be involved in all the intricate details of home management. However, every woman, we believe, has a desire to be a part of the leadership team with her husband. This is part of the oneness that God has designed for marriage. Eve was originally called alongside Adam to help him oversee the daily responsibilities of tending the Garden. How much more so has God designed that a Christian husband and wife who are one in Christ serve together in leading the family?

4. Submission does not mean a wife should indulge in sin because her husband demands it.

When Paul stated that "wives should submit to their husbands in *everything*" (Eph. 5:24), he certainly did not mean they should violate God's revealed will. There are times when Christian wives must say, just as Peter and the apostles did in Jerusalem, I must "obey God rather than men" (Acts 5:29).

But a word of warning! Before a Christian wife resists her husband's wishes, she must make sure that what he wants her to do is indeed a violation of God's revealed will. It's very easy for any one of us to justify resistance on the basis of predetermined notions and convictions that are not based on Scripture but rather on tradition and culture and even selfishness.

Furthermore, every Christian wife needs to understand what God meant when He stated to Eve and all her sisters, "Your desire will be for your husband" (Gen. 3:16). The word "desire" can mean "an attempt to usurp or control." Keeping that in mind, we can paraphrase the last two lines of this verse as "You will now have a tendency to dominate your husband, and he will have a tendency to act as a tyrant over you." Just as every husband has a natural tendency to be selfish and to want to control and dominate his wife, so every wife, as a result of sin, has a natural tendency to challenge the authority of her husband.[8] Consequently, when a wife feels that her husband is asking her to do something that she should not do because it violates her conscience, it's at this point that she needs trusted and mature women who can help her evaluate these situations biblically and objectively. This is certainly one reason why Paul instructed Titus to teach the older women to train the younger women to be submissive to their husbands. Included in this process is a need to help them discern when submission is a violation of the will of God in other aspects of the Christian life.

5. Submission does not mean a wife must subject herself to physical and psychological abuse.

Unfortunately, some women are married to men who are so self-centered and evil in their actions that it is impossible to cope with the problems. No matter what these women do to try to be submissive wives, their husbands only take greater advantage. Men like this are sick, spiritually and psychologically. At this point, a Christian wife needs to seek help and advice from the elders and pastors of her church. She cannot bear the problem alone.

Such a situation is really a matter for church discipline. Jesus clearly taught that all Christians have a right to seek help when other Christians are sinning against them. This certainly includes husbands and wives who simply form a smaller social unit within the church. Consequently, we could interpret Jesus' statements as follows:

If your brother [your husband] sins against you, go and show him his fault, just between the two of you. If he listens to you, you have won your brother [husband] over. But if he will not listen, take one or two others along, so that "every matter may be established by the testimony of two or three witnesses." If he [your brother or husband] refuses to listen to them, tell it to the church [the legal assembly of elders or pastors]; and if he refuses to listen even to the church, treat him as you would a pagan or a tax collector (Matt. 18:15-17).

However, we need to issue a word of warning! Some women find it very easy to rationalize and project themselves as unappreciated martyrs, but in reality they have not been obedient to Scripture. They have defined submissiveness by their own standards, not by the Word of God.

On the other hand, there are Christian wives who take the biblical exhortation to submit so seriously that they end up becoming enablers, actually encouraging their husbands to continue in their sins. When this happens, it's time for tough love, and most women who are facing these situations definitely need wisdom from other mature Christians to be able to discern what actions should be taken.[9]

Thinking and Growing Together

The following questions are designed for group discussion after reading and studying the content of this chapter:

- Can you think of situations when a wife may be truly submissive to God's will in her life but has difficulty submitting to her husband? Why might she have this difficulty?

- Why would a Christian woman use the biblical truth that she is "one in Christ Jesus" (Gal. 3:28) with her husband as a basis for arguing against her husband's headship, or leadership, in her marriage?
- When does the freedom for a wife to express her opinions and feelings to her husband become inappropriate and a violation of the principle of submission?
- What are some biblical exceptions for a wife *not* to submit to her husband? How can she handle these exceptions biblically?
- If a wife is in an abusive relationship, how can she deal with the situation in a biblical way?
- About what can the group pray for you personally?

Set a Goal

Write out one goal you would like to achieve as a result of this study.

Endnotes

Chapter 1

1. C. F. Keil and F. Delitzsch, *Commentary on the Old Testament, The First Book of Moses (Genesis)*, trans. James Martin (Peabody, MA: Hendrickson Publishers, 1996), p. 56.
2. Ronald Allen, *The Majesty of Man* (Portland, OR: Multnomah Press, 1984), pp. 145-147.
3. For Anne's full story, see John and Anne Paulk, *Love Won Out* (Colorado Springs, CO: Focus on the Family Publishers, 1999).

Chapter 2

1. James Montgomery Boyce, *Romans*, vol. 4 (Grand Rapids, MI: Baker Books, 1995), p. 1912.

Chapter 3

1. When outlining the qualifications for selecting men to serve as deacons, Paul inserted a paragraph that is puzzling, even for Bible translators (see 1 Tim. 3:11). Here he mentioned four qualifications for women. The Greek word he used for women, *gunaikas,* can be used to describe any adult woman who is married, who has never been married or who is widowed or divorced. Most Christian leaders over the centuries have not accepted the interpretation that Paul was referring to deacons' wives. Rather, the most common understanding is that he was addressing the qualifications for women who also serve as deacons.
2. Here Paul was using the term "man" in a generic fashion, including both men and women.
3. For an exegetical treatment of Paul's phrase "the husband of but one wife," see Ed Glasscock, "The Husband of One Wife Requirements in 1 Timothy 3:2," *Bibliotheca Sacra*, vol. 140 (July 1983), pp. 244-257.
4. See note 1.

Chapter 4

1. Herbert Lockyear, *All the Women of the Bible* (Grand Rapids, MI: Zondervan Publishing House, 1991), p. 102.

Chapter 5

1. Name order *is* significant in Scripture when determining prominence in particular situations. Matthew made this point emphatically by actually

saying, "These are the names of the twelve apostles: *first* [*protos*], Simon (who is called Peter)" (10:2). This Greek term actually means "foremost, either in time, place, order, or importance" (Wigram and Green, *The New Englishman's Greek Concordance and Lexicon* [Peabody, MA: Hendrickson Publishers, 1982], p. 765). Also in the book of Acts, again and again, Luke mentioned Peter's name first when Peter and John ministered together in the early days of the church (see Acts 3:1,3,11; 4:1,3,7,13,19,23). Note also that Peter repeatedly was the primary spokesman (see 2:14-40; 3:4,6,12-26; 4:8-12; 5:3-9).

We see this same pattern with Barnabas and Paul. As this ministry team began its first journey, Barnabas was definitely the primary spokesman (see Acts 13:2,7). However, when they reached Paphos, they reversed roles. From that point forward, Paul is mentioned first in almost every instance, indicating his prominence as a spokesman (see 13:9,42,46,50; 14:1; 15:2). However, when they arrived in Jerusalem to resolve the circumcision controversy, Barnabas became the primary spokesman (see 15:12), probably because Paul was still remembered among Jewish believers in Jerusalem and Judea as a persecutor.

Chapter 6

1. Herbert Lockyer, *All the Women of the Bible* (Grand Rapids, MI: Zondervan Publishing House, 1991), p. 149.

2. The Greek word translated as "dear" in 1 Thessalonians 2:8 is *agapetos*, which actually means "beloved" or "dearly loved" (Wigram and Green, *The New Englishman's Greek Concordance and Lexicon* [Peabody, MA: Hendrickson Publishers, 1982], p. 27). Paul was definitely referring to an agapao-type love, which he and other New Testament writers used frequently to describe their relationship with fellow Christians (for examples, see Rom. 1:7; 2 Cor. 7:1; Eph. 6:21; Phil. 4:1; Col. 4:7; 2 Tim. 1:2; Jas. 1:19; 1 Pet. 2:11; 1 John 3:2,21; 4:1,7,11).

3. The word *sophronizo*, translated as "train" in the *New International Version* of the Bible, literally means to make one sober, to restore one to his senses; to moderate, control, curb, discipline; to admonish and exhort earnestly (Wigram and Green, *The New Englishman's Greek Concordance and Lexicon*, p. 823). In the *New American Standard Bible*, Titus 2:4 reads, "That they may *encourage* the young women to love their husbands."

Chapter 8

1. Herbert Lockyer, *All the Women of the Bible* (Grand Rapids, MI: Zondervan Publishing House, 1991), p. 24.

2. Wigram and Green, *The New Englishman's Greek Concordance and Lexicon* (Peabody, MA: Hendrickson Publishers, 1982), p. 823.

3. Ibid.

4. Ibid.

Chapter 9

1. Wigram and Green, *The New Englishman's Greek Concordance and Lexicon* (Peabody, MA: Hendrickson Publishers, 1982), p. 11.

Chapter 10

1. Billy Graham, introduction to *The Henrietta Mears Story*, by Barbara Hudson Powers (Westwood, NJ: Revell, 1957), p. 7.
2. Ethel May Baldwin and David V. Benson, *Henrietta Mears and How She Did It* (Ventura, CA: Regal Books, 1966), pp. 42-43.
3. Ibid., p. 43.

Chapter 11

1. Herbert Lockyer, *All the Women of the Bible* (Grand Rapids, MI: Zondervan Publishing House, 1991), p. 46.
2. Lange, quoted in Herbert Lockyer, *All the Women of the Bible*, p. 46.
3. Lockyer, *All the Women of the Bible*, p. 47.
4. Wigram and Green, *The New Englishman's Greek Concordance and Lexicon* (Peabody, MA: Hendrickson Publishers, 1982), p. 2.
5. Bible translators have made different judgments in translating "agathos." Some connect it with *oikouros,* the word that is translated in the *New International Version* as "to be busy at home," so that together they are translated as "good homemakers" (see the *Holman Christian Standard Bible*). Others treat the word separately. We have followed this more common approach of classifying "agathos" as a separate quality of maturity (see the *New King James Version* and the *English Standard Version*).

Chapter 12

1. Herbert Lockyer, *All the Women of the Bible* (Grand Rapids, MI: Zondervan Publishing House, 1991), p. 94.
2. Donald Davidson, quoted in Lockyer, *All the Women of the Bible*, p. 99.
3. S. C. Humphreys, *The Family, Women and Death* (Ann Arbor, MI: The University of Michigan Press, 1993), p. 48.
4. Ibid.
5. Otto Kiefer, *Sexual Life in Ancient Rome* (London: Constable and Company, 1994), p. 31.
6. We realize that some interpret "head" to mean "source." However, we believe this interpretation is very difficult to substantiate. To learn more about this discussion, see *Recovering Biblical Manhood and Womanhood*, eds. John Piper and Wayne A. Grudem (Westchester, IL: Crossway Books, 1991).
7. William J. Webb, *Slaves, Women and Homosexuals* (Downers Grove, IL: InterVarsity Press, 2001), p. 269.

8. *The Nelson Study Bible* (Nashville, TN: Thomas Nelson Publishers, 1997), footnote to Genesis 3:16.
9. To explore this subject more, see James C. Dobson, *Love Must be Tough: New Hope for Families in Crisis* (Portland, OR: Multnomah Press, 2004).